CHORAL MUSIC: TECHNIQUE AND ARTISTRY

CHARLES W. HEFFERNAN
University of Massachusetts

PRENTICE-HALL, INC., *Englewood Cliffs, New Jersey 07632*

Library of Congress Cataloging in Publication Data

HEFFERNAN, CHARLES W.
  Choral music.

  Bibliography: p.
  1. Choral singing—Instruction and study.
I. Title.
MT875.H33   784.9′6   81-17759
ISBN 0-13-133330-5   AACR2

40,746

Editorial/production supervision
    by Dan Mausner
Cover design by Dawn Stanley
Manufacturing buyer: Harry P. Baisley

Printed in the United States of America

10 9 8 7 6 5 4 3 2

ISBN 0-13-133330-5

PRENTICE-HALL INTERNATIONAL, INC., *London*
PRENTICE-HALL OF AUSTRALIA PTY. LIMITED, *Sydney*
PRENTICE-HALL OF CANADA, LTD., *Toronto*
PRENTICE-HALL OF INDIA PRIVATE LIMITED, *New Delhi*
PRENTICE-HALL OF JAPAN, INC., *Tokyo*
PRENTICE-HALL OF SOUTHEAST ASIA PTE. LTD., *Singapore*
WHITEHALL BOOKS LIMITED, *Wellington, New Zealand*

to
HOWARD SWAN

Dean of American Choral Conductors

CONTENTS

FOREWORD

Howard Swan

Choral Music: Technique and Artistry is not just one more volume concerned with the problems of the choral conductor. Charles Heffernan is a specialist both in the fields of music education and choral music. For many years he has been associated with colleges in this country and Canada and has had ample opportunity to test his theories and procedures in the classroom and the choral rehearsal. He writes as he teaches, with unusual clarity of expression and a logical presentation of factual material followed at intervals by summation and review. Because each problem is defined in understandable terms and suggestions for its solution follow in practical sequence, Heffernan's book will be useful as a text for a class in conducting or as a worthwhile addition to the library of a choral conductor.

This book is not a manual which treats conducting patterns, nor does it deal with organizational techniques, lists of repertoire or other peripheral concerns. The author's principal premise is that every choral conductor must also be a teacher and the contents of this volume are written in their entirety with this objective in mind. Heffernan discusses the conductor as musician, listener, technician, leader, as a teacher of voice, and as one who deals surely and effectively with choral techniques. Finally, and much of this material is new in idea and practice, he suggests ways by which choral artistry may be defined, rehearsed and achieved.

Each section of this volume is provided with one or more memorable topics which draw the attention of the reader and in turn are most helpful to the thoughtful conductor. Necessary conducting techniques are discussed in Chapter 2. Chapter 3, titled *Vocal Technique*, contains step by step procedures dealing with breathing, support, freedom, and resonance. Professor Heffernan's proposals will conform easily with any type of vocal pedagogy to which singers may have been exposed. The chapter ends with 60 exercises designed to solve a variety of vocal problems.

Heffernan classifies all choral techniques (Chapter 4) under the five categories of pitch, rhythm, tone, dynamics and text. Each of these musical attributes receives adequate attention in terms of "why" and "how" and here again appear many vocalizations to help each singer overcome any particular difficulty. The "50 guidelines for efficient rehearsals" which review all of the material presented in the preceding pages are practical and effective.

It is in the area of "artistry" that Charles Heffernan makes his most important contribution to choral thought and practice. He asserts that any choir which has mastered fundamental techniques under proper leadership "can advance into the artistic stage of choral performance." To be ready for such an experience the conductor and the chorus first must study and interpret correctly according to the *stylistic* demands of each composition. This requirement should be accompanied by an understanding of the *phrasing*, with particular emphasis upon the intensity and sense of forward motion inherent in each musical statement. Finally, the singers must learn from members of the acting profession how one becomes *personally involved* with a particular situation presented by a text and its musical setting. Heffernan writes of motivation and the need to imagine and fantasize. Such skills are learned by explanation, demonstration and many hours of practice. Most importantly, the singers must establish within themselves the belief that they actually were present when the event, experience or musical commentary first took place or was conceived.

The author cautions that always in performance there must be a balance between technique and artistry; "a part of the mind must continue to be objective." He then follows his usual procedure by ending this section with excellent guidelines for the "development of belief."

Charles Heffernan has chosen with care the subject matter which appears in his book. Constantly he explains, summarizes and challenges the choral conducting profession. All is accomplished with a logical pattern of instruction accompanied at times by flashes of good humor. The reader will find that familiar materials often receive from this author a treatment which is different and thought provoking. At the same time there is much here that is new. Thus, it is a personal pleasure to recommend *Choral Music: Technique and Artistry* to my colleagues and friends.

ACKNOWLEDGMENTS

This book would not have been possible without the patient indulgence of the innumerable choristers who have rehearsed and performed under my direction during the past thirty years. Through analysis of their fervent or feeble responses, together with methodical study, I gradually synthesized the art of choral conducting as presented in these pages; my thanks to all of you who may peruse this book.

At the risk of offending some of my favorite choirs by omission, I would like to express my special appreciation to the members of the University of Toronto Concert Choir who, during my tenure as their conductor, assisted me in solidifying most of the concepts presented herein. Memories of our performances of the great choral masterpieces will always occupy an important place in my thoughts.

I am also most appreciative of the valuable criticism of Harold Haugh and Howard Swan, who, in addition to giving me years of personal guidance, read, corrected, and contributed immeasurably to this manuscript. Without your encouragement, it would not have been completed.

Finally, to my wife Margaret and daughter Priscilla, whose loving support during years of rehearsals and concerts have enabled me to retain my sanity and to write this book, my undying gratitude!

Charles W. Heffernan

"Conducting is very funny.
It's not just beat. It's
not just eye contact. It's
not just how I look. But I
think it's how I feel inside,
and orchestra feels it." *

Seiji Ozawa

*from an interview with Louise Sweeney, *The Christian Science Monitor.* (2/23/79)

CHAPTER ONE
A ROUTE TO CHORAL ARTISTRY

The scene is familiar to all choral conductors. It is the first meeting of the annual festival, Choruses in Conjunction. From a wide geographic area, members of community, church, and college choirs have come together for two days of intensive rehearsals and a public concert under the direction of a renowned guest conductor. Many preparations preceded this first rehearsal: a program of challenging compositions was long ago selected; all the choristers have their own music which has been thoroughly marked according to directives received by the various conductors of the individual choirs involved; the notes have been learned, and several regional rehearsals have already taken place. All is as prepared as it possibly could be, and a strong sense of eager anticipation fills the auditorium. The responsibility for the success of the festival is about to be passed to the guest conductor.

The General Chairman of the festival, who has been very busy during the last hour getting everyone seated in the proper place, is now giving the customary introductory talk preceding the appearance of the maestro. His many contributions to the field of choral music are mentioned—compositions, editions, recordings, and written articles on conducting. He is widely experienced as a guest conductor of choral festivals, and his own choir is internationally recognized as a standard for all choirs everywhere.

The chairman concludes, "Ladies and gentlemen, the conductor of this year's Choruses in Conjunction—Robert Roger Dove!"

From the wings briskly steps the maestro. To the accompaniment of warm applause he shakes hands with the rehearsal pianist, then bows graciously to the observing officials, guests, and directors of the various choirs. He turns to the singers, and a few words of appreciation are spoken. Then the rehearsal begins with the final chorus of Cantata No. 140 by J. S. Bach, *Wachet auf, ruft uns die Stimme.*

During the next ninety minutes, all those present are witness to that phenomenon which occurs when a great conductor is on the podium. Mere patterns of organized vocal sound which hitherto exhibited little coherency slowly and steadily form into an artistic whole. Pulsing rhythms, flowing lines, variety of tone color, and dramatic aspects of the text begin to appear at appropriate points; it seems as if life itself is being pumped into the notes. The music begins to take shape, and everyone present knows that throughout the subsequent rehearsals, a continuous unfolding of choral artistry will be demonstrated. The climax of the festival will occur right on schedule in the final concert, and the ovation will be tremendous.

To watch Maestro Dove rehearse is to behold creative artistry itself. His conducting gestures, graceful and concise, guide the singers through preparations, attacks, and releases. Although his movements are definitely on the conservative side, his entire body is involved in clarifying the rhythmic components of the music. The score is open on the stand before him, but he rarely consults it. The singers can always see his face, which shows a remarkable variety of emotions. He is as a man possessed, projecting with great intensity the technical and artistic aspects of the music. There is no doubt that he has totally absorbed the compositions. Indeed, he seems to be the very personification of the works themselves.

His rehearsal procedure is a masterful plan of steps toward definite goals. He adjusts the intonation, tidies a rhythmic problem, and clarifies the diction. He calls for and obtains a more appropriate tone color by demonstrating several voice production principles. He elucidates the text by reading and explaining certain passages. He balances the dynamics to enable the essential line to be heard. As a master psychologist, he builds up the confidence of the choir with praise, scolds it for inattention, builds tension with intense dynamics and tempi, relaxes the atmosphere with humor. Like a skilled surgeon, he operates constantly at the peak of his powers of concentration.

The reaction of the observers scattered throughout the auditorium is remarkable for its variety. There are, of course, the Dove disciples, an enthusiastic group of choral conductors to whom the maestro is The Way. Most of them are his students; others have followed him from festival to workshop renewing their energies, inspiration, and techniques. All the disciples see themselves as the someday successor to Dove.

Other conductors present, to whom Dove's rehearsal style is less familiar, are busy taking notes. With the hope of finding some new choral techniques with which they can improve their own choir, they record his vocal studies, his explanations of diction, his rhythmic pedagogy, his witticisms. Although there is occasional skepticism on points of interpretation, tone, or other matters, all agree that Dove knows what needs attention and how to remedy the problem. Many of them remark that observing these rehearsals is exactly what they need at this point in their careers.

No conductor is without critics, and several are present for this first rehearsal. They will not be seen again until the final concert, at which time they will express, with faint praise, their reserved appreciation of Dove's work. Some of these critics feel that they themselves could do at least as well as Dove if they had better singers in their choirs. There are many objections: the tone of the Renaissance compositions is too warm; the Baroque music is being taken too fast with undue emphasis on the rhythm; the concern for diction is destroying the line in the contemporary works. Some of the critics are still miffed that their choice for a conductor for the festival was bypassed in favor of Dove. "If only Sir Paul Woodcock were here today," they comment, "then we would have a *real* musician. Dove, of course, is acceptable, but he is essentially a showman!"

Festivals such as the one just described are quite common in North America today. They serve to generate considerable enthusiasm for choral music, especially at the high school level. At times, a remarkably artistic performance takes place at the conclusion of the festival. There are also those performances that everyone would prefer to forget!

With the many opportunities that choral directors have to witness fine conductors, or to attend workshops or master classes in conducting, or to have their choirs adjudicated by some of these same conductors, would it not be reasonable to expect that a superior level of choral performance would exist throughout this continent? That this is not the case is a regrettable fact. Why are so many choral conductors unable to profit from the excellent instruction they receive? Why do countless school, church, and community choirs continue to sound so poor year after year? In the midst of all this inspired instruction, is there a missing Rosetta stone, whose absence reduces all this valuable information to a disjointed mass of technical devices? I believe this is the case.

To the general observer, it appears that master conductors of choral ensembles move confidently through a maze of correctional, inspirational, and musical techniques. They seem to have an inexhaustible supply of solutions to problems and an uncanny ability to select exactly the right procedure at the right time. Under this plan, which indeed seems to move from inspiration to inspiration, the choir makes steady improvement.

Conductors of lesser ability and experience will often try to imitate a master conductor by utilizing procedures and techniques observed at workshops and festivals. They may emulate the maestro's podium manner and even don similar rehearsal attire. Aspiring conductors may attach themselves to a particular school of choral singing (straight tone, covered tone, school for screamers, or other) and attempt to create in their own choirs a carbon copy of the original group. Their rehearsals are frequently characterized by a nervous application of technique after technique delivered with the desperate hope that things will somehow get better. Their rehearsals often end with a sense of frustration, for no one knows what has been accomplished or what is yet to be done.

It seems to me that the major factor which distinguishes the work of a master conductor from that of a novice is not so much that the maestro has a wealth of information to impart, but rather that a definite goal is in mind at all times. Like a fine chess player who plans far beyond the move made at any given time, the master conductor is always working step by step toward points of perfection which may not be achieved until far down the rehearsal schedule. Great conductors are always operating with a plan; they know what they want to hear and work toward that end.

Novice conductors, in contrast, have no well-defined goals in mind, except possibly a glorious concert! They have, therefore, no route to follow and no plan of action. Their rehearsals are pointless and frustrating for all concerned. They may then be accused of lacking ability or "fire from heaven." In retaliation, they may attempt to shift the blame to the choir members, condemning them as uncooperative or untalented.

All conductors need a plan, a sense of direction in the rehearsals. They must have both short-term and long-range goals in mind as well as routes that will take the choir to the accomplishment of these goals. There are, of course, several ways to get to any destination. A traveler may go from Toronto to Los Angeles by way of Chicago, St. Louis, and Phoenix. One could also go first to Vancouver, then to Seattle and San Francisco, or even to Miami, New Orleans, and Houston. But there would be little point in heading first for St. John's, Newfoundland!

Starting out in the wrong direction is exactly what confused conductors are doing when they scold their choir for singing out of tune without ever having taught the singers the basics of a well-supported tone. A choir is sometimes admonished for not delivering the drama of the composition when the diction is so bad that almost no words are intelligible. The classic loss of direction is the frustrated scolding at a dress rehearsal for not standing with good posture!

It is this lack of well-defined goals and ignorance of the step-by-step process toward accomplishment of those goals that cause so many directors of choirs to fall short of what they might achieve. These conductors are often good musicians possessing considerable talent and knowledge, but because they lack a grasp of the principle of first things first, their rehearsals become a floundering mass of technical applications poured forth in a haphazard manner. They may, by chance or by good luck, produce decent results, but more often than not they fail to bring their choir to anything approaching an artistic choral performance.

There is a logical progression of instruction in vocal and musical matters which will lead a choir to heights of artistic excellence. The purpose of this book is to present this *continuum* of choral music experiences in a manner that will enable both the beginning and experienced conductor to determine the stage of advancement of a chorus and to proceed from that point. The continuum is the result of my thirty-some years of conducting choirs of every possible level of accomplishment and from my teaching and observation of scores of conductors who run the full gamut from total failure to smashing success.

The plan of progress toward choral artistry is depicted below.

Level I

The conductor:
   the musical qualifications, training, and experience
   the conducting technique
   the ear for choral sound
   the personal qualities of leadership
   the preparations for rehearsals

Level II

Vocal technique:
   the conductor as teacher of voice
   the necessity for vocal instruction
   the basis of good singing: posture, breathing, support, freedom,
      resonance
   special problems of sopranos, altos, tenors, basses
   vocalises for beginning, intermediate, and advanced singers

Level III

Choral technique:
   auditions
   seating the choir
   development of the choral body
   techniques of pitch—training the ear
   first rehearsals of a new work
   perfecting the pitch sense
   appropriateness of the repertoire
   techniques of rhythm—the inner sense of pulse
   techniques of tone—activation, articulation, color
   choral dynamics
   the text—vowels, diphthongs, consonants

amalgamating the choral techniques—achieving the "learned note" level

Level IV

Choral artistry:

the relationship to technique

moving beyond the notes

the essence of music

style

subtleties of rhythm and dynamics

phrasing

motivation, involvement, outward manifestation

choral drama

choral performance and the theater

CHAPTER TWO
THE CONDUCTOR: THE KEY TO CHORAL ARTISTRY

The most important single factor in the development of a choral organization is its conductor. A choir may consist of a number of very good singers; it may have excellent rehearsal facilities and a large budget for music, concerts, and tours. It may have a long history of successful choral activities. It will not, however, reach or maintain a high artistic level of performance with a conductor who is musically deficient or lacking in qualities of leadership. This chapter will discuss the tools a successful choral conductor needs and will suggest ways to go about acquiring these tools. The ten sections are not presented in any order of importance; they should all receive careful thought. A notable characteristic of successful conductors is their ability to grow, to improve. It is hoped that this chapter will provide a stimulus for self-examination and regeneration.

KNOWLEDGE OF MUSIC HISTORY AND CHORAL REPERTOIRE

A wide knowledge of the history of music is absolutely essential for choral conductors. They should be familiar with the works of great composers from all periods and should have experience in performing in the styles appropriate to the time of the compositions. Many conductors have a limited knowledge of the repertoire and are therefore unable to bring to their choir the great variety of music it deserves. Too many conductors specialize in one area—Renaissance, Baroque, or commercial popular—and fail to educate their singers and audiences. Conductors must continually broaden their knowledge of the repertoire, *neglecting no period or style.* Among the most glaring weaknesses in this regard are choral directors who are not familiar with, and therefore pretend disinterest in: (1) less well-known composers of any period, (2) contemporary music, (3) secular music, and (4) music by so-called "popular" composers. The conductor who dismisses the music of, say, George Gershwin as insignificant is guilty of snobbery, has a closed mind, and is headed for trouble.

A conductor who has had the benefit of university training in music probably will have taken several general courses in music history. Concentrated study in history of choral music, church music, or singing is also often available. However, the growth of a conductor's repertoire seems to come most often from hours of studying the complete collected works of a particular composer, from examining the great historical editions of music such as the *Denkmäler der Tonkunst in Oesterreich* or *The English Madrigal School,* and from perusal of new publications found in catalogs, at festivals and conventions, and at workshops and music stores. Every successful conductor has a vast library of choral music acquired through years of sifting through the enormous quantities of scores available. Constant work with the compositions in this library is essential for the conductor's personal growth. Through studying, playing, and singing scores, inspiration is renewed. One of the worst things conductors can do is to limit their study to the compositions under rehearsal at a particular time. Conductors, get your library organized. Build it up. Work with it constantly.

The following steps may be helpful in developing a wider knowledge of choral repertoire.

1. Select a general history of music such as Grout's *History of Western Music.* Read it through and make a list of all the composers mentioned. Try to find some choral compositions by each composer. Do you know, for example, any choral pieces by Dittersdorf?

2. Select a favorite composer and, with the aid of reference books, compile a list of the choral compositions. Study a large number of these compositions and play recordings of them. Ask yourself questions such as, "How much do I really know about the choral music of Mozart?" Do not be put off by the fact that your choir cannot, at this time, perform these works; we are concerned here with your personal growth. Through this growth you may expand the capabilities of your singers, or you may move to a new situation.

3. Select a composer about whom you know very little. Try to obtain information concerning this person and his or her choral works. Do you know contemporary composers such as Natalie Sleeth, Violet Archer, John Beckwith, and Henry Leland Clarke? Get some of their compositions into your library and study them.

4. Study and rehearse some compositions that are in a style that is less familiar to you. If you always perform anthems with organ accompaniment, try some easy a cappella works. If you have never utilized instruments with your choir, do something with a small group of players. Rehearse some folk songs or a Broadway medley with your church choir. Study some compositions written in twelve-tone technique or with a taped, electronic music accompaniment. Branch out! Be different!

5. Establish good relations with several music stores in different parts of the country. These companies are usually willing to send you material on approval. Discipline yourself to spend a certain amount of time each week, month, or year seeking new compositions for your library.

6. At least once a year attend a workshop, reading session, or choral music conference. Buy all the music you hear. Bring it home and study it regardless of your reaction to it.

7. If you are inclined to give repeated performances of certain favorites, put them away for a time. You may conduct "Fairest Lord Jesus" or "Elijah Rock" very well indeed, but let them rest. Force yourself to do some new works; this action is necessary for your well-being.

8. At least once a year give a première performance of some choral work. You have a responsibility to contemporary composers.

KNOWLEDGE OF MUSIC THEORY

A thorough grounding in the theory of music is necessary if conductors are to comprehend the structure of the works they are directing. This knowledge includes skill in harmonic and formal analysis and a study of counterpoint, absolutely necessary for the understanding of Renaissance and Baroque music in particular. Choral conductors are, indeed, teachers. In addition to perfecting the notes that your choir sings, you must constantly enlighten the singers regarding the construction of the composition and guide them in grasping the work as a musical entity. Conductors must be keenly aware of essential and nonessential material as they seek to achieve balance and clarity with their ensembles. It is only with this deep knowledge of contrapuntal and harmonic technique that the conductor can lead a choir to an *understanding* of the composition.

This in-depth grasp of music theory may be likened to the knowledge displayed by a skilled mechanic who, in repairing a badly functioning engine, disassembles the mechanism, cleans and inspects each part for imperfections, then puts all the pieces together again to form a smoothly running whole. A significant part of any music rehearsal follows exactly this same process. In a kind of composition-in-reverse approach, the conductor tears down the faulty section or movement and lays bare the badly tuned leading tone or accidental, the incorrectly executed rhythm, or a set of notes dynamically out of balance. Having polished the essential fugue subject or other important line to brilliance, the conductor then slips it into place among supportive counter-material and gradually reconstructs the composition.

The ability to do this work is largely dependent upon proficiency in music theory or analysis, for one must first locate the problem, extract the faulty component, repair it, put it back into place, and then listen to hear if the correction was successful. At the same time, if any educational development is to take place in the choir, the conductor must be able to explain lucidly what is being done. Failure to pinpoint a problem and to correct it in an enlightening manner is a prominent characteristic of an inept choral director.

A conductor who needs further study in theory and analysis should seek a good teacher. A concentrated period of study as outlined by Julius Herford in *Choral Conducting—A Symposium* (pages 177–230) would prove to be enlightening to most conductors. Lacking the opportunity for such in-depth study, the student could apply Herford's procedures to works being rehearsed at that time. In the process, a self-motivated, deeper examination of the composition will be brought forth. Later in this chapter we will consider the entire procedure for preparing a score for rehearsal.

PERFORMING ABILITY

Although there have been some notable exceptions, most successful conductors possess considerable performance ability on an instrument or as a vocalist. This skill is important for the choral director. One frequently encounters conductors who at one time were quite capable as performers but, for one reason or another, stopped practicing. A conductor needs a place to practice creative artistry, and, lacking unlimited rehearsal time with an ensemble, can utilize his or her instrument or voice to refuel the inspirational fires. Of course, advancing age brings a certain amount of veneration, but conductors should guard against substituting baton technique too soon for instrumental or vocal practice. Ensemble problems of interpretation or artistry are often most clearly elucidated for a choir by an apt vocal or instrumental demonstration. Indeed, conductors may win increased allegiance or respect from their singers by their ability to make these exemplifications.

Continue to practice. Dig into new repertoire. Take lessons. Especially beneficial to the choral conductor is the study of an orchestral instrument. Play in an ensemble. You will be a better conductor for your labors.

KNOWLEDGE OF VOICE

A choral conductor must have a thorough understanding of the human voice. Lack of knowledge on this point is a severe handicap. True, choral conducting posts are often held by organists, pianists, or instrumentalists. In such situations, the conductor is entirely dependent upon the presence of knowledgeable singers in the choir if any kind of acceptable choral sound is to come forth. The conductor who is deficient in vocal information is lost when dealing with problems of out-of-tune singing, bad tone, or poor articulation. You need not be a great vocal artist, but you must be able to listen to a singer, isolate and evaluate any vocal problems you hear, and know how to correct these deficiencies. Choral conductors also need all the experience they can obtain with foreign languages—Latin, German, Italian, French, and Spanish, to begin with.

There is no short route to this essential information. Many excellent books on singing are available, and the serious conductor will study them. However, reading is no substitute for substantial instruction from a good teacher. Choral conductors need all possible study in voice with an emphasis on basic vocal technique. They need experience singing in good choirs where they can observe knowledgeable conductors working with vocal problems. High quality vocal and choral experience may well be the most important aspect of a choral conductor's training.

KEYBOARD SKILL

It is not *essential* for a choral conductor to play the piano; however, it is a most valuable tool to have in one's hands, first, as a way of evaluating new scores, and second, as a means for developing interpretations. Conductors may occasionally find themselves without a competent rehearsal pianist, and it is very helpful if they can cover such emergencies. When performing choral works that include extensive solo parts, conductors usually must spend extra rehearsal time with these singers alone. If they can play for these coaching rehearsals, time will be saved in arriving at a cohesive interpretation.

If it is at all possible, choral conductors should develop some ability at the piano. Sometimes the greatest benefit is obtained from study of keyboard harmony, chording, and improvisation, rather than the traditional "thumbs on middle C" approach.

ABILITY IN SIGHT-SINGING

At both rehearsals and concerts the conductor should stand before the choir, where he or she can clearly communicate by means of conducting gestures, facial expressions, and body movements. In rehearsals, there must also be explanations and demonstrations of vocal and choral techniques. Conductors should therefore be able to sing the lines of the composition to illustrate what they want. Unless they have the ability to sight-sing the particular part needing attention, they will have to learn each part thoroughly at the keyboard before coming to rehearsals. Even then, they must be able to locate pitches in any part easily and deliver them to the singers as they correct errors. To rely on the rehearsal pianist or organist to do this is not wise; it is far better for the singers to hear the lines sung. Conductors who are unable to sing correct pitches and rhythms for the choir lose rehearsal time and, in turning to the pianist for constant help, relinquish a portion of their communication with the ensemble. Such an act may also cause the choir to lose confidence in the maestro.

A choral conductor should therefore develop as much skill as possible in sight-singing. Unlike the other requirements for conductors mentioned in this chapter, sight-singing ability can be developed without the assistance of a teacher. Two things are necessary: the conductor must be convinced of the need for this skill, and he or she must be willing to devote time to regular practice. Several graded books of sight-singing studies are available and are listed in the Bibliography. Regular practice of these materials will yield rich rewards to the conductor who is deficient in this area.

A conductor-in-training should carry a tuning fork or a pitch pipe and use it several times a day. Try to develop the ability to sing a certain note without reference to the instrument. Practice until you can sing any interval up or down from any note. Remember, the most atonal music still requires the performer to sing specific intervals. Also, buy a good metronome and practice with it regularly. Perfect your ability to maintain a tempo and to subdivide with absolute accuracy.

CONDUCTING TECHNIQUE

A choral director should have a secure technique in conducting. In rehearsals it is often possible to obtain good results by merely demonstrating or explaining your wishes to the ensemble. In concerts, however, the director must convey directions to the choir largely by gesture, and, although some conductors have gone far on the strength of a highly personalized system of signals not unlike cheerleading, it is far better if directives can be delivered with clear, traditional patterns of preparation, attack, release, and nuance. Good conducting technique is vital if the maestro is to work as a guest director or at a festival, where there is usually insufficient time to acquaint the forces with a personal style. If instrumentalists are to perform with the choir, the choral conductor must be prepared to rehearse them with precise and meaningful gestures. Orchestral musicians are inclined to be rather intolerant of a choral conductor whose downbeat consists of a karate chop preceded by a provocatively lifted eyebrow.

Prospective conductors should have had considerable experience during their student years in leading groups of singers and instrumentalists. In these studies, the emphasis should be upon the development of clarity in the gesture, precision in attacks and releases, and awareness of possible sub-tleties in the pattern. The emerging conductor should guard against too radical a departure from the traditional patterns coupled with the onset of a personal style. Every conductor can profit from objective criticism of his or her directing by the singers, by a knowledgeable friend in the audience, or from refresher courses or workshops. Study some of the conducting books listed in the bibliography.

The following points, which are the basis of my own conducting tech-nique evolved over a long period of time, may assist you in more clearly conveying your wishes to your ensemble.

1. The conductor must constantly provide a model for the singers. At all times, maintain a posture of commanding presence. Instill this characteristic into your choir members. Your posture, bearing, and attitude are reflected by your ensemble. Stand tall with your feet well together. Do not spread your legs as if you were setting out to plow the fields!

2. Except for very small chamber choirs (which probably do not need a conductor anyway), conduct your forces with a baton. Far greater precision is possible than with the bare hand, expressive as the latter is held to be. Most of the great conductors use a stick.

3. Insofar as possible, stand up to conduct. If you are so tired or ill that you require a stool, cancel the rehearsal and go home. Stand with dignity as befits your station.

4. Perfect and trust your preparatory beat. Make it say everything possible re-garding tempo, intensity, mood, and tone. It is the most important and most neglected of all conducting motions. Conducting is essentially a series of preparations coupled with a flow of reminders of previous instruction.

5. Privately, before a mirror, practice conducting the pieces you are going to rehearse until your gestures are absolutely clear. If at any time your conducting technique falters, no transmission of musical directives can take place. Your singers are then deprived of your guidance and may go off course.

6. Look at your singers almost all the time. If you do not, they will not be with you. You may not do more than occasionally glance at the score.

7. Do not conduct *notes*, even with the most juvenile or inexperienced choirs. Move cleanly and smoothly from beat to beat with as little extraneous motion or subdivision as possible. A baton in your hand helps with this point.

8. Do not sing with your choir. Rather, listen.

9. Keep the pattern low, at about the level of the diaphragm, and well in front of you. This position constantly draws the singers' attention to the power center of the body and helps to produce a firmer tone. A high pattern or fluttering hands at eye level (as when one is conducting from an organ bench) are conducive to the development of a screechy sound.

10. Regardless of the dynamic level, work to maintain *vitality* in the beat. Each ictus must have a feeling of lift, of forward motion.

11. Beware of continuous large gestures; a refined, intense, willful motion is usually more effective. Smaller gestures require greater concentration from your singers; therefore, they remain in closer communication with you.

12. You also conduct with the face and eyes; show emotion with the body. These factors are more important than flailing arms. Occasionally, try to conduct

your choir without using your arms, relying entirely on facial and bodily movements.

13. A fermata has no pulse; therefore, usually, there should be no beat. Arrest the pattern and give a feeling of continuity in the tone with the body or the left hand.
14. *You* may feel the music powerfully within you; vivid pictures may pass through your mind as you conduct. In spite of these motivations, however, your beat must always be clear.
15. Never allow yourself to go out of control. Wild gyrations on the podium are usually distracting rather than inspiring.

AN EAR FOR CHORAL SOUND

A successful choir conductor must have an ear for choral sound. It is quite possible for an excellent orchestra or band conductor to fail when working with a chorus; the notes may be correct but the choir simply does not *sound*. It does not do for the choral conductor to merely accept the sound produced by the choir. It is necessary to have a clear concept of what a choir *should* sound like and then know how to produce that sound with the singers before you.

There are at least two important factors that have a bearing on this point. First, the conductor's total lifetime vocal and choral experience will supply the musical memory with a great variety of aural events. The sound of children's choirs, high school choirs, church choirs, college glee clubs, and professional choirs, to name but a few, will impress the musical consciousness with sounds that will be periodically recalled. Conductors who lack long and deep experience in listening to choral sounds will find themselves deficient when attempting to develop a satisfactory sound with their own groups. Their ears simply lack appropriate and sufficient experience.

Although it is most valuable when developing the choral ear to have had years of magnificent experience performing in and listening to fine choirs, it is never too late to start. Begin at once to train your choral ear. Go to rehearsals and programs of various choirs. Attend a workshop or convention of choral enthusiasts. Buy some recordings by several different choruses. Try regularly, possibly even daily, to exercise your choral ear and to feed your choral memory bank. When listening, do not merely take a tonal bath in the wash of tones. Listen perceptively. Get below the surface of the sound and analyze the less apparent aspects of the performance.

A good conductor must be keenly sensitive to minute variations in pitch, volume, and tone color. The difference between mediocrity and excellence in choral performance is very often characterized by *subtle* adjustments in these three factors. All too often, a conductor will have a good ear for pitch in the middle and upper voices but seem oblivious to tone clusters in the bass section, or one's concept of a dynamic scheme may consist only of a general loud and soft level with no nicety of gradation in between.

Learn to listen for tiny details, for when you are building your own choir you will find that most vocal and choral improvements are, at first, *very small*. For a time, you may be the only person who can hear these small changes in tone, pitch, or volume, but it is vital that you detect these sprouting buds, point them out to your singers, and encourage the nurturing of these growths. Too many conductors stop listening to other choirs or listen only to convince themselves that their own choir is better. In so doing, they limit their own growth and fall far short of their potential as leaders of choral forces.

The second factor in regard to an ear for choral sound is that choral conductors must work to develop the ability to hear *within* themselves the ideal choral sound for any composition they are studying. They must be able to *imagine* the sound of the perfect ensemble performing the particular work. In creating this model within the imagination (and it must be a detailed creation, not merely a general impression), conductors give themselves a goal toward which they can move. Then, with a refined choral ear, they are able to take the actual sounds obtained from the singers before them, and, with creative rehearsal techniques, work to resolve any disparities. The two creations may never reach perfect alignment, but having an ideal sound *toward which* one is moving will do much to stabilize the enigmatic course so many conductors take in their rehearsing.

It is therefore obvious that the refinement of the choral ear and the growth of the choral imagination are inseparable. The imagination must begin with details that have been fed to it by the ear and then go on to sublimity. As the ideal performance is created within, the ear is stimulated and made more acute. Having begun to train the choral ear to listen for details, you should try to create the perfect performance within. Begin with a short, simple composition you know well. Try to imagine the ideal soprano, alto, tenor, and bass sound. Put them together in different combinations, and finally create the ideal whole. Then try to hear the entire composition through. Recreate it in your thoughts in several different ways. Select the version you feel is best and polish it further. Study of this sort will give a firmer direction to your rehearsals.

PERSONAL QUALITIES OF LEADERSHIP

In addition to these eight musical requirements that conductors must possess, there are several other more personal factors that will determine one's success or failure as a leader of choral ensembles. These items are fully as important as the musical credentials; they all work together, and the absence of any one will eventually become painfully apparent.

By the very nature of the occupation, a conductor must be a leader of people. Indeed, he or she must not only lead but must also simultaneously create in the ensemble an eagerness to be led. Without this fervor in the singers, the conductor's labors will be compounded, and a high level of artistry will not be reached. Whether they wish it or not, conductors constantly present themselves as models for their forces. On the simplest level, a director's posture and overall bearing are reflected by the singers. However, his (or her) influence upon the choir far exceeds such elementary points. His attitude toward music, the arts in general, and life itself will be communicated. The seriousness with which he views his tasks, the depth of his preparation for rehearsal, the demands he makes upon himself, his promptness, and his approach to people will be impressed upon the ensemble and later returned to him. The conductor should be very aware that even such an item as the tone of voice in giving directions has a great impact on everyone present. When drilling a passage, a command of "Again," given in a droning monotone, will produce a strikingly similar response from the choir, whereas a vibrant "Once more!" will be reflected by a much more vital tone. It does indeed behoove would-be or active conductors to take constant stock of themselves and objectively ascertain what kind of model, visually, intellectually, morally, and socially, as well as vocally and musically, they present regularly to their chorus.

As conductors become aware of the enormous influence they exert, a great strain may be placed upon the psyche. There is no doubt that a conductor is always under great pressure; the thought that large numbers of people are constantly looking to one for leadership can produce tension. Conductors gradually come to realize that they are viewed by their ensembles with a curious mixture of love, respect, admiration, fear, and dislike. They govern and lead their forces by a unique combination of inspiration, authority, persuasion, threats, and, at times, something akin to violence. Regularly confronted by such a gamut of emotional and sociological batterings, a conductor may give way under the strain and become autocratic, overbearing, petty, and generally difficult to get along with. One may miss rehearsals, fail to keep appointments, and act irrationally. The whole pattern can culminate in a general breakdown of emotional stability and health. Alcohol, drugs, and riotous living offer little real help. Somehow, by means of intellectualization, rationalization, meditation, prayer, psychotherapy, or vigorous physical exercise, an active conductor must learn to deal with the hazards of the occupation. You must simultaneously love the work and grow in it. You either advance or fall back.

It is well for aspiring conductors to be aware of the toll such a career may extract. Its rewards can be many; the great conductors have been notably long-lived. Conducting is not an easy, routine, or peaceful occupation. It is a calling to a great responsibility. It has proved to be too much for many people.

A conductor must overcome any personal sense of timidity in taking action. Outward evidence of insecurity, shyness, or fear in dealing with either the music or the performers will immediately be communicated to the members of the ensemble and drastically reduce the effectiveness of the conductor, regardless of other strong points. Performing ensembles of good quality very likely include several members with strong personalities. These members, not necessarily with malice, are not above harassing or trying out a conductor in a multitude of ways. Singing wrong pitches, singing too loudly, being inattentive, looking bored, looking amused, sitting or standing with slovenly posture, singing with blank faces, and asking inane questions tinged with innuendos are some of the arrows these pranksters have in their quivers. The conductor must be prepared to deal with these problems; some suggestions are: in-depth musical preparation and scholarship, humor, tolerance, withering glances, and a touch of steel, in that order. The first two items should, ideally, suffice, and a conductor who finds it necessary constantly to harangue, threaten, browbeat, or impose sanctions on the ensemble should thoughtfully evaluate the entire situation. He or she may be in the wrong position or even the wrong profession.

The personal relationship between the conductor and the performers may be very close or nonexistent. Some outstanding conductors are addressed, even in rehearsals, in the most familiar terms; outside of working hours these conductors socialize freely with the ensemble members. Other conductors prefer to have only the most businesslike and impersonal contact with their ensemble. No advice on this point is of value; either approach can work, depending on the situation. The key point in these sometimes knotty circumstances is that a conductor must never do or permit anything to take place in a social situation that will diminish the respect due in rehearsals or concerts. A conductor, to a great extent, succeeds in the occupation in proportion to the degree of respect and cooperation received from the players and singers. One wins respect from the ensemble in many ways—by musicianship, by enthusiasm, by organizational and executive strengths, by the ability to instruct. A conductor *is* essentially a teacher, a person with knowledge and a strong commitment to people. Between master and pupil there is a dividing line, albeit faint. Over this line, *in both directions*, there should be free passage of information and inspiration, together with expressions of friendship, concern, and love. However, the line must never be erased. Loss of respect for the conductor because of an untoward development in a social situation can be a very serious matter. Playing favorites, gossiping about the singers, or permitting undue familiarities can terminate a conductor's effectiveness with the group. Neither animosity nor personal fondness can be permitted to influence a conductor when working with the members of the choir.

A SENSE OF RESPONSIBILITY: PREPARING FOR REHEARSALS

Long before the conductor steps before the choir to rehearse a composition, the work should have been studied in great depth and its literary and musical content been totally assimilated. The conductor must *ponder* the work and make every attempt to ascertain what the composer was trying to express. He or she must be prepared to explain what the work is about. During the course of rehearsals, the conductor may have a change of mind on certain points; many great conductors experiment and revise their first conceptions. However, any conductor who learns the score along with the singers is failing in a sense of responsibility.

The following steps may serve as a guide for this preparation. With a pencil in hand—

1. Study the text. Read it aloud. Be certain of the correct pronunciation of every word; consult a dictionary regularly. If it is in a foreign language, you must know not only the general meaning of the text, but also a precise English equivalent of each word. Learn everything you can about the source and background of the text.
2. Insofar as your pianistic ability permits, play the voice parts and the accompaniment, if any. Bring as much of the printed page into sound as possible to gain a general impression of the music. Locate the major climax and points of secondary interest. Determine the form.
3. Sing each part. Learn it at the keyboard if necessary, but practice until you can sing any line with confidence. Study the work from the linear standpoint. Find any points of repetition or imitation. Mark the difficult leaps.
4. Do two-part study at the keyboard. Play the soprano and bass, soprano and alto, alto and tenor, tenor and bass, soprano and tenor, and the alto and bass. As you are doing this, *imagine* the ideal sound of each section. Mark dissonances or other potential problems.
5. Study the harmony. Play all the parts together as best you can. Notate the keys. Circle the accidentals. Know what the composer is doing at all times.
6. Read everything you can about the composition and the composer.
7. Restudy each part; try to hear it in relation to the whole. Circle every tempo, dynamic, and interpretive mark on the page. Leave no printed indication untouched. Look up any unfamiliar terms.
8. In a quiet place, practice conducting your supreme, imaginary ensemble through the work. Try to hear within you every detail the page reveals. Perfect your conducting gestures.
9. Listen to *several* recordings of the composition. Do not play a single recording over and over again. Conduct these recorded ensembles. Stand up; put the score on a stand; prepare and cue each entrance; watch yourself in a mirror. Memorize. Free yourself from the score.
10. Put the composition away for a time. Give your subconscious a chance to develop the music.
11. Review steps 1 through 9. You should now be prepared to begin rehearsing.
12. Demand a great deal of yourself. Then you have the right to demand much of others.

In the case of a work with orchestra, follow these same procedures. In addition—

13. Buy your own full score and mark it thoroughly.

14. Buy your own instrumental parts. Check them against your score. Align rehearsal letters or numbers.

15. With the help of a string specialist, if necessary, put in the bowings before the first rehearsal.

16. Go through the brass parts and mark down the dynamic levels. Draping a cloth over the music stands will also cut down brass resonance and assist in balance problems.

Needless to say, preparation of this sort cannot be done on the way to the first rehearsal or even the evening before. Depending upon the complexity and duration of the work, a full preparation as described here requires from several days to a year or more. Especially important is the period required for step 10; during this time the composition will grow and mature in your thought. You will then be ready truly to conduct the music, not merely to beat time while notes are sung. Your choir expects leadership from you; do not fail them.

CHAPTER THREE
VOCAL TECHNIQUE

The instruments of a choir are the voices of the singers. Just as it is impossible for a fine orchestra to be formed from an assemblage of badly played, ill-adjusted instruments, so is it impossible for a choir to achieve any degree of artistic or even technical success if the singers are not in command of their voices and utilizing them to their full potential. Almost everything else that follows in this book is predicated upon the thesis of this chapter: *choir members must be taught how to sing.* Conductors of choirs that aspire to a high level of artistic excellence must, therefore, view themselves not only as leaders of organizations but also as teachers of vocal technique. Although members of the choir may be studying voice privately, they are under the tutelage of the conductor for a much longer period each week. The director's influence, vocally, can be extensive, and he or she must accept the responsibility of this position of leadership.

The choral conductor may be blessed with a large number of knowledgeable singers, but it is more likely that there will be a wide range of vocal abilities present. In any case, an assemblage of highly trained singers will in no way ensure a choir with a magnificient sound; it is only through the efforts of the conductor that variance in tone can be unified. It therefore becomes the responsibility of the conductor to instruct the choir members in the basics of vocal technique, giving a foundation to those lacking any knowledge of singing, and, it is hoped, expanding the understanding of the voice in those with more vocal experience. As almost all choirs will have a few good singers, it is obvious that the weak singers need to be strengthened so that unification may be achieved within the sections of the choir. Until this leveling out of ability has been achieved, there is very little that can be accomplished toward the building of a fine chorus, for either the strong voices will dominate the entire ensemble, or the poor singers will drag down the good ones into a quagmire of bad tone, faulty intonation, sloppy rhythm, and other choral problems.

It cannot be stressed too strongly that the weak singers must be strengthened with gentle, persistent instruction in how to sing, and that it is the duty of the conductor to do this work. Choir singers often cannot hear their own vocal deficiencies, and for a choral educator to neglect these problems is to shirk a primary responsibility; it will not do to dismiss singers as untalented or stupid—they must be taught. It is in this regard that choral rehearsals differ most markedly from instrumental rehearsals. Although the orchestral conductor advises on bowings, fingerings, or other technical matters, nowhere near the amount of time is spent on individual, personal instruction such as the choral director must give to the choristers. This point is frequently misunderstood.

Most conductors begin their rehearsals with a warm-up period. It is during this time that instruction in elements of singing can be easily given, for the conductor can concentrate on one or two aspects of vocal technique and evaluate the progress that is being made. In addition, it is vital that throughout the entire rehearsal the conductor keep an ear tuned for any problems that are not essentially choral ensemble problems but rather are indications of faulty singing by individuals. The conductor must not waste the time of the entire choir on a vocal problem that can be more easily solved with some attention at a sectional, small group, or even individual coaching session.

What are the elements of vocal technique? Essentially, there are three clearly distinguishable factors to be studied and remembered at all times when a person is singing.

1. A steady, constant, controlled supply of air under pressure.
2. A relaxed, freely floating, coordinated set of neck, throat, jaw, and facial muscles.
3. An understanding and development of resonance in the voice. This third element almost always develops naturally when the first two components are operating in correct relationship to one another.

It may seem that to reduce the art of vocal technique to the three items listed above is an oversimplification of the countless theories of singing expounded upon in the multitude of books that have been written during the last four centuries. These three components do not include concern for registcrs, breaks, lifts, placement, or any of the other mysteries of singing so dear to certain schools. Nevertheless, any conductor who can teach the choir to master the three basics of singing set forth above will find that the singers are well equipped to handle almost any problem of choral technique that may arise. After these factors have been thoroughly mastered, the conductor with special vocal interests or terminologies can go on to them with the certainty that the singers are well prepared.

It is important that conductors studying this book do not assume that all choir singers understand and practice these three components naturally and habitually. It is amazing how many singers with considerable private study in voice do not sing with adequate, controlled breath supply and constantly show tension in their throat. Their tone frequently has little resonance or carrying power. The bulk of time in their voice lessons is given over to study of operatic roles or arias or interpretation of the great song cycles, rather than the building of vocal technique, which may be dismissed as being too elementary or inartistic for inclusion in private instruction. The deficiency in technique may not even be recognized until a singing career has been well launched. Then, the inevitable sore throats, cracking, and loss of high tones make it all too painfully clear that a castle has been built on sand and that the voice student must go far back in his or her studies and build or repair the foundations. Sometimes the singer cannot do this remedial work, for the voice has been seriously damaged.

In a similar manner, the choral conductor who does not realize the importance of the three components of singing will, in a perfunctory manner, run the choir through a few warm-ups and then plunge into the repertoire for the next concert. The notes are pounded into the ears of the singers, and rehearsals ensue at a high level of inspiration. Frequently, even the warm-ups will be discontinued. After considerable time, and often as a public performance is about to take place, it will become apparent to singers and conductor alike that the melismata will never become clearly articulated, that the tenors will never achieve the high notes, that there will never be a clean pitch in the bass, that the altos will continue to sound like sopranos who smoke, and that the entire ensemble sings with a dull, monochromatic tone. The conductor may plead, threaten, or pass the whole mess off as a bad experience, but basically the director has failed the choir. Too much was assumed; the singers did not know how to use their voices, and *the conductor did not teach them.* Curiously enough, conductors seem prone to repeat this error in choir after choir and year after year. Often-heard excuses for this shameful conduct are: "I don't have time to teach voice production," "These guys are too old (too young) to improve their voices," "My singers are pros; they know all that stuff," "I'm a conductor, not a voice teacher," or "We're not interested in technique; we want to sing."

The three components of good singing can be easily and quickly demonstrated by the conductor-teacher, although admittedly it requires considerable time, effort, and patience before a choir as a whole *habitually* applies these techniques to the repertoire being rehearsed. Warm-ups or preliminary exercises at the beginning of the rehearsal may get the voices operating well, but there is frequently great difficulty in carrying the knowledge gained in the warm-ups over into the study of the music. Conductors must, therefore, call upon their skill as teachers and constantly draw attention to specific points in rehearsals that are related to vocal technique. A wise conductor will select portions of the repertoire and construct vocal studies upon these fragments, thereby having the singers improve their technique and study the music simultaneously. Indeed, a mark of a good choral conductor is the ability spontaneously to create corrective rehearsal techniques as they are needed.

One reason so many singers, solo and choral alike, are slow to appropriate and fully utilize these fundamentals of singing is the fact that the first two items are naturally, physiologically, and psychologically in conflict with each other. Sometimes, even though the principles have been well practiced during rehearsals, the pressure and excitement of public performance will crack the discipline that has been gained. Singers will stand with bad posture, drop their support, strain for high notes with tight throats, and commit all sorts of other vocal atrocities. The conductor may be partially responsible for this slip in technique, for in the enthusiasm to produce excitement, intensity, or fervor during the performance, he or she will overconduct or overstimulate the choir to the point where the would-be joyful noise unto the Lord assumes more the character of a bacchanal. It is therefore essential that the elements of good singing be studied not only in the opening warm-up exercises but also at every appropriate point in the rehearsal. The conductor must remain firm on these points until the choir has completely assimilated them and constantly applies them. In our basic plan of first-things-first, it is impossible to overstress the importance of developing a set of secure singing habits that will stand by the singer in any situation and under the direction of any conductor.

Let us now examine in detail each of the components of vocal technique.

A STEADY, CONSTANT, CONTROLLED SUPPLY OF AIR UNDER PRESSURE

This component includes the processes of posture, breathing, and support. The singers must be taught how to stand and to sit. They also must learn the mysteries of abdominal or diaphragmatic breathing, the sensation of the air supply under pressure, and the method of controlling this air as it passes through the larynx. Most books on singing devote a large part of the discussion to this item, and the knowledgeable conductor will study them all, in spite of a number of conflicting opinions.

The following points and exercises have been used to teach this component to hundreds of singers in choirs and in private lessons. Some of them are my own creation but many are the results of years of discussion, reading, and observations of other conductors. They are notated here with my thanks.

Posture

Many singers do not stand properly. Bad posture can be seen throughout most choirs, and it is a special problem in high school choruses, where teenagers stand first on one foot, then the other, with the opposite knee collapsed. The following exercises will help give singers the proper stance.

Stand firmly, with the feeling that you are *gripping* the floor with both feet. Feet should be about a foot apart, right foot about 6 inches ahead of the left foot and turned slightly out; the body weight is evenly divided between the balls of the feet; little weight should be felt on the heels. The body then becomes poised as if for ascension.

FIGURE 3.1

With feet in this position, firm the leg and pelvic muscles, reach both hands high over the head, and, without bending at the knees or waist, sway the body forward and backward. Then, keeping the same position, sway from one side to the other and, finally, sway in a small circular motion.

If the choir members can do this, they probably are standing with good singing posture, with a feeling of constant vitality. Another device that is fun is to form pairs of singers and have one person try to push the other off a vertical axis. I sometimes urge my singers to stand as if resisting an 80-mile-an-hour wind, or experiencing a rapidly decelerating subway train. However it is accomplished, singers must stand tall with firm foot, leg, and pelvic muscles. This position is the foundation upon which the breathing apparatus rests.

Good standing posture makes possible maximum capacity for air in the thorax. Standing correctly, with chest lifted, the chin in, and the elbows away from the sides of the body, gives the singer adequate control of the breath flow. Furthermore, maintaining these various components of good posture creates in the singer a *commanding presence,* an indispensable element in fine choral performance.

The choir must also learn to sit properly. After the standing position is well established, have each singer sit down on a good, solid chair. The body weight is now transferred from the feet to the buttocks, not to the back, which must remain straight and not in contact with the back of the chair. I usually illustrate to the choir my own sitting posture which I have developed during thirty-some years as an equestrian and long-distance motorcycle rider.

FIGURE 3.2

The back is curved slightly in. The head sits *atop* the spinal column, not in front of it.

The choir needs also a *relaxed* sitting position, to be used during explanations and discussions or when other sections are rehearsing. Under these conditions, the singers can sit back and rest against the back of the chair. Extending the feet forward and crossing the ankles is also restful. Crossed *knees* are an abomination and should not be permitted. Moving from this relaxed position to an alert sitting position can be accomplished in a moment, and the choir should learn to assume the correct position the instant the conductor calls for active vocal participation.

Do not neglect the posture of your choir singers. The effect of good posture can be easily shown by a little experiment. Ask the choir to sing a well-resonated chord while standing with excellent posture. Then while continuing the singing, have the choir sit down properly. Observe that there is very little change in the tone of the singing. Finally, have the choir continue to sing and ask them to slouch down in their chairs and cross their knees. Note that it is virtually impossible to retain a good tone under these conditions.

Breathing

There is considerable confusion in the minds of most singers regarding correct breathing for singing. Choir members can, of course, breathe, but can they breathe for singing? Frequently they do not understand the proper uses of the diaphragm. Lacking this understanding, they use a lifted chest breathing instead. When asked to take a deep breath, they raise their shoulders, throw out their chest, and suck in their stomach; in so doing they create a large amount of tension, which is almost always transmitted to the voice.

Singers should be made aware of the different ways air may be taken into the lungs and learn which of these ways is most appropriate for good singing. First, they should observe *clavicular* or chest breathing. This is the breathing people utilize when their bodies require a large amount of oxygen during and following strenuous physical exercise. It is characterized by a heaving, pumping motion of the chest together with a rise and fall of the shoulders. Clavicular breathing should not be used for singing. It produces tension, which causes bad tone, cracking notes, and excessive vibrato or wobble. Many choir singers use clavicular breathing almost exclusively; older singers who have used it for a long time will clearly show the results—shaking heads and quivering chins and throats.

Correct breathing for singing is produced when *intercostal* or rib breathing is combined with *diaphragmatic* or abdominal breathing. This is the way the body takes in air when sitting or lying in repose. It can be clearly demonstrated by a singer lying in a supine position with hands clasped behind the head. It will then be seen that the abdomen protrudes upon inhalation and retracts when expiration takes place. With the choir seated in a relaxed position, singers can experience this correct breathing technique by extending the abdomen and attempting to *expand* the body around the waistline. There is usually no problem with pushing out the stomach but many people have difficulty expanding around the base of the rib cage. Some teachers use the terms "belly breathing" or "balloon breathing" in teaching this concept. A good test for proper expansion around the waistline is to place the hands on hips, swinging the hands around so that the fingertips are lightly touching near the lower part of the backbone. The thumbs should be under the rib cage at the sides. Try expanding around the waistline so that the fingertips separate.

When the conductor is assured that everyone understands this correct breathing process, the choir members should be asked to stand and to inhale deeply, taking in air through both the nose and the mouth. Be sure that there is obvious expansion of the abdominal and waist area and that there is no lifting of the shoulders, an indication of clavicular breathing. Singers who have difficulty with the concept of deep abdominal breathing are sometimes benefited by inhaling through the nose only, as if smelling a faint fragrance of a flower. Practicing nose breathing may help the singer to learn to take in more air. The choir should practice taking breaths *rhythmically* as in the following exercises:

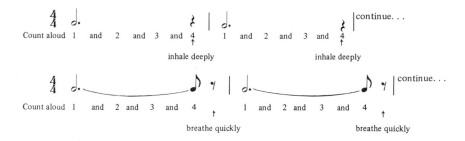

In doing these exercises, the choir should learn to take in a full supply of air on either the quarter or eighth rest. Especially important is the *catch breath,* as in the second exercise above. There should be little or no sound during the inhalation. A gasping intake of air is an indication of a closed throat. Be sure that the air is taken in at the tempo of the ensuing counting; this action will ensure success in breathing at the conductor's preparatory beat.

Combine these rhythmic breathing exercises with pitch exercises as follows:

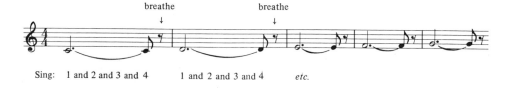

In spite of the great importance of inhalation, of taking full, deep breaths rhythmically, the really vital thing in singing is the exhalation. A big breath taken in and expended on two notes is of little value. The singer must work diligently to control the outflow of air, *gradually* emptying the lungs.

The instant inhalation has been completed, exhalation normally begins. It is the exhaled air that passes through the larynx and produces sounds. For proper singing, this exhaled air must be passed through the larynx under complete control in regard to pressure and rate of flow. This control is produced by the abdominal muscles and by the intercostal muscles which pull the ribs inwards. The use of these muscles, especially those of the belly area, are essential to proper singing. They help produce a tone that is said to be well *supported*.

Support

Many choir singers do not understand support or proper expiration of air. Having taken in breath with the clavicular muscles, they simply allow the chest to fall and use their swallowing muscles to control the flow of air through the larynx. Such a singer is often said to be singing from the throat. Throat singing is very common in children's choirs, high school choruses, and any other choral group that is conducted by a person without vocal knowledge or an ear for good choral sound. A choir consisting of throat singers may have a fairly decent sound in simple literature that does not require high notes, rapid articulation, or much dynamic contrast. Choirs of throat singers are usually flat in pitch, especially on higher notes or descending passages. They sing with a lifeless tone, although it may be raucously loud, and they lack crisp diction, because of the inability to articulate rapidly. Unsupported tone is one of the most common faults in choral singing. Teach your singers to inhale properly and to support the outgoing flow of air.

To have the choir experience proper use of the abdominal muscles while exhaling, ask them to *bark* loudly as would a large dog. You might even bring a big dog to a rehearsal. Have the singers observe that at the moment of the bark, the muscles used for inhalation (the diaphragm and the intercostal muscles that cause the outward expansion of the base of the ribs) are operating in opposition to the exhalation muscles (abdominal and intercostal muscles that pull the lower ribs in). The exhalation muscles are exerting a slightly greater force than the inhalation muscles; therefore, support is being created and can be easily seen as well as felt. Correct posture and barking can demonstrate easily the principle of supported tone. Male singers seem to succeed in this activity more easily than females, possibly because of the larger muscles. A person who has difficulty grasping the concept of diaphragmatic breathing can often accomplish the action better while sitting down.

Once the bark is clearly operating, try a sustained bark or howl. Observe that the momentary opposition of the inhalation and exhalation muscles during the bark is now a continuing condition as the howl ensues. The abdominal muscles remain firm and slowly press back into the body as the air supply is expelled. Have the singers observe that the sense of pressure does not diminish as the end of the breath approaches and that the dynamic level of the howl is directly related to the abdominal pressure, not to the tightness of the throat.

A singer who can bark and howl is prepared to sing passages of staccato or articulated notes essential to vigorous choral work. A test of the various singers' understanding and proper use of supported tone is as follows:

Ask the singer to articulate clearly with a vigorous abdominal action on each of the first four notes. Transpose the exercise up and down chromatically and gradually increase the tempo. The notes should be crisp and well in tune. Singers who produce a breathy, weak tone from the throat do not understand support and will make very little contribution to the choir. Teach them how to do it and insist that everyone sing with supported tone at all times.

The following exercises may be helpful in developing a sense of support in singers who lack it. At the same time care must be taken not to create *oversupport;* sharpness of pitch and objectionable tremolo will result.

Preliminary exercise: buzzing loose lips. Take a full breath. Exhale and try to make the loose lips flutter as children do when playing with toy cars and trucks. Also practice long *hissing,* maintaining a steady pressure from the abdominal muscles.

1. With the mouth open, sing the word *hing* loudly, with a vigorous abdominal thrust. Move immediately to the *ng* and sustain it with strong support. Working in pairs, feel each other for the firm muscles just below the bottom of the rib cage. Carry the pitch down five tones without losing the intensity. Try for a *slight* crescendo.

2. Invert exercise 1.

Staccato vocalises are excellent for determining if support is being established. Without proper support, the following exercises will have a breathy, undirected sound. Work to develop crisp articulation.

Transpose upward by half steps; gradually increase the speed. Articulate.

These exercises will undoubtedly suggest possibilities for others which the conductor may devise. All vocalises should begin in the middle part of the voice and be transposed up and down to cover a wide range. Vocalises that move upward (4) should be alternated with ones that move downward (5). Vary the speed. Insist upon clean pitch. Have various sections of the choir vocalize alone while others listen. Do two exercises simultaneously, such as sopranos on 6 and basses on 7. Do this work regularly but only for short periods.

A RELAXED, FREELY FLOATING, COORDINATED SET OF NECK, THROAT, JAW, AND FACIAL MUSCLES

This second aspect of good voice production is directly related to the factors of good posture, breathing, and support as discussed above. Occasionally, singers find it very difficult to stand tall with a firm posture and lifted chest while at the same time relaxing the shoulders and the muslces of the neck and throat. One often sees singers striving for excellence with a good posture and understanding of support but, unfortunately, showing a very tense neck and clenched jaw, together with tight facial muscles twisted into unbecoming grimaces or frowns. It is impossible to produce good tone for solo singing or choral work until complete freedom rests atop a firm foundation. These opposing factors must be clearly explained and then regularly practiced, until a balance of strength and relaxation is achieved between the two areas of the body.

Tension in the wrong places is frequently the result of two incorrect aspects of vocal production mentioned previously—use of clavicular or high chest breathing and use of the peristaltic action of the throat (swallowing muscles) to operate the voice. In the first case, use of the large muscles of the chest and shoulders while inhaling will almost always tense the muscles of the neck and jaw. The tension then continues because the interaction of the diaphragm and abdominal muscles (support) was not established. The chest then falls during exhalation and the throat muscles are used to control the flow of air through the vocal folds. The ensuing tight, colorless sound, so typical of badly taught choirs, is no joy to hear and is beyond any kind of refinement. In our plan for a continuum of choral experiences leading to artistry, it should now be apparent that the fundamentals of posture, breathing, and support are absolutely essential to any kind of success with a choir.

Relaxation and freedom from tension can be taught with a number of exercises.

1. As a choir, stand and face to one side rather than toward the conductor. Massage the entire neck area and shoulders of the singer standing before you. After a few minutes, turn to face the other way so that a reciprocal workout can take place.

There are many benefits to be derived from this activity. First of all, a certain amount of hilarity always arises; laughter induces freedom from tension. If the singer whose neck is being massaged can be encouraged to utter long glissando, relaxing sighs of *ah, oh,* or *ee,* the hilarity may be increased, together with a good sensation of free tone from an open throat. A second psychological benefit from this activity is that an increased sensation of belonging to the section or choir develops. A good choir is an integrated sociological unit; the members must have confidence in one another and be "in touch." It should be pointed out here that this exercise is primarily for relaxing tense muscles; it is not group therapy or a sensitivity session. A singer does not have to be a registered masseur to recognize and loosen tight neck muscles, and some people develop considerable skill in providing relief from this common problem. Of course, this activity must be used with discretion. If excessive embarrassment or inhibition becomes apparent, or if a breakdown of discipline develops, the exercise is of no value. However, in most situations such a session can deliver large physiological and psychological benefits. Try it.

2. Roll your head around in as many directions as possible and consciously attempt to keep the neck free from tension. Working in pairs, place hands on each other's necks to check for stiffness. You should have the sensation that only enough energy is being expended by the neck muscles to keep the head from falling forward or to one side.

3. Say several times the colloquial affirmative, *m-hm*.[1] Drop the jaw as low as possible with the lips still lightly touching, as with hot food in the mouth. Nod the head up and down gently as if in agreement with a friend. Work to eliminate any feeling of tension. When total freedom is felt, try sustaining the *hm* on any low pitch. The result should be a tension-free hum. Continue the hum, *checking that posture and support are being maintained.* Drop the jaw further, so that the lips part, and sing on the same pitch the vowel *ah.* The result should be a freely produced tone from an open throat. Repeat the exercise, starting with *m-hm* and changing to *huh-huh* with open mouth. Move to *yah-ha,* then to:

yah   hah   hah   hah   hah   Start at any low pitch

The above sequence of instruction can be very beneficial to singers who have never experienced the sensation of a fully open throat. It is also revealing to conductors who will discover that some of the singers have never supported at all and have spent all their choral singing days producing pinched tones from the throat.

4. The sensation that accompanies the incipient stages of a yawn is a most valuable aid in demonstrating a relaxed, open throat. Experiment individually and in pairs with the producing of loud, vulgar, zoo-like yawns. The mouth should be opened wide with an accompanying sound which glissandos from a very high pitch to the lowest notes of the voice.

---

[1] The great benefits of *m-hm* were first brought to my attention in Kenneth Westerman's *Emergent Voice* (Ann Arbor, Mich.: Edwards Brothers, Inc., 1947).

The above is another hilarious exercise which can yield both psychological and physiological benefits. Singers must understand the absolute necessity of abandoning muscular and nervous tension and must make conscious efforts to let go and relax. Always in singing there must be a kind of inner yawning sensation. Indeed, yawns, sighs, and laughs all contribute to a relaxation of the spirit. As Father Finn used to say, "Keep the Choristers relaxed and in good humor."[2]

A word of caution is appropriate here regarding the often-heard admonition to "Just relax!" Vitality is the result of muscular tensions; without these tensions we would collapse into a flaccid heap on the floor. What we must eliminate are the *deleterious* tensions. Good singing is the result of great muscular activity of the right sort combined with *specific* relaxations. Good singing *sounds* effortless, easy. When properly done, good singing *feels* easy. *But,* good singing is neither effortless nor easy; it is the proper harnessing of great expenditures of energy. Urging your singers to "Just relax!" without explanation, can be quite harmful.

In general, the sensation of relaxation will be assimilated more quickly than the complexities of breathing and support. Although there are opposing factors in these two components of good singing, they also are closely related, and a singer who breathes and supports properly will probably find few difficulties with relaxation, once it has been clearly explained and demonstrated. When breathing, support, and freedom from tension are well coordinated and habitually practiced by the singers, the path is open for the development of resonance, a crucial factor in the production of good vocal tone.

AN UNDERSTANDING AND DEVELOPMENT OF RESONANCE IN THE VOICE

The basic sounds produced by the vocal cords are faint. For them to develop fullness, richness, and carrying power, they must be amplified, activated, and resonated. The techniques of breathing, support, and relaxation, if carefully carried out by the choral conductor, will provide a basis for the development of resonance. There are also a few additional points that should be understood if singers are to utilize the full potential of their resonating areas. Without resonation, a choir cannot produce any kind of brilliance in the tone, and an unresonated forte or fortissimo by a choir is no joy to hear—it is merely a loud, unpleasant sound.

There are, essentially, three main areas of resonation in the singing mechanism: the pharynx or throat, the mouth, and the nasal cavities. See

[2]William J. Finn, *The Art of the Choral Conductor* (Evanston, Ill.: Summy-Birchard Company, 1960), I, 36.

Figure 3.3. These three areas must be under the control of the singer at all times. When they are being used correctly, together with proper breathing and support, the maximum potential of the choir singer is being realized.

The primary factor in achieving resonance is the creation of *space.* There must be room for the basic vocal sounds to "roll around," for want of a better term. As this space is opened, fullness and resonance are created. Of the three resonating areas mentioned, two can be consciously controlled in regard to size or space—the pharynx and the mouth. The singer can do nothing about the size of the nasal cavities but *can* control the opening from the throat to this cavity.

Although the mouth is not the most important resonating area, it is the easiest area in which to demonstrate the creation of space. With the inexperienced singer, the first sensations of improved resonance can be felt most easily in the mouth. Choir singers must often be encouraged and taught how to open their mouths; without an open mouth the sound is diminished. How frequently you see singers striving for fullness in their tone, yet maintaining a mere slit with the mouth, through which the sound must come! Different dynamic levels and vowels affect the degree to which the mouth must be opened.

To produce space in the mouth the singer must learn to drop the jaw very low, *without tension.* You might ask the singers to open their mouths as if preparing to take a large bite from an enormous, juicy apple. Choir members who have sung for years with tight jaws will find it necessary to work diligently on this aspect of good vocal production. Exercises on rapidly

FIGURE 3.3

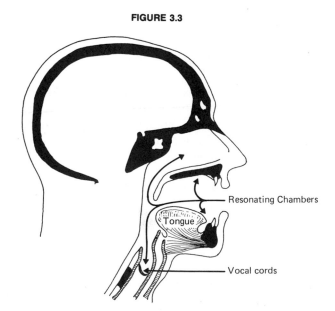

Resonating Chambers

Tongue

Vocal cords

reiterated spoken *bah, yah, pah,* and *mah,* in which the jaw moves freely from a closed to a fully open position, are useful. Singers should also practice moving the jaw freely from side to side. As these jaw-movement exercises are performed, care must be taken to see that the muscles of the face and neck are absolutely free from tightness. Also to be guarded against is the rather common tendency to open the mouth laterally (←→) rather than vertically (↕). The ensuing, slit-like opening then emits an undirected, unresonated tone sometimes referred to as being "spread" or diffused. A loose, well-opened jaw, coupled with the sensation of an inner yawn, will do much to develop a singer's tone; the improvement will be apparent immediately.

With the jaw well down and relaxed (not pulled back) the way is prepared for further work toward an open throat, a constituent of good vocal production considered desirable by most teachers of singing. If you reexamine the resonating areas in Figure 3.3, you will see that a clear passageway from the vocal cords upward to the mouth and into the nasal cavities is essential to free resonance. Two factors sometimes prevent this free movement of tone: the tongue and the soft palate.

The tongue is a rather unruly mass of muscles and tissues capable of a multitude of positions. As the back and sides of the throat are relatively stationary, it is apparent that the back of the *tongue* is the major factor controlling the size of the throat opening. Any action that causes the tongue to bunch up at the rear of the mouth will cause the throat to close. Singers sometimes develop strange concepts of what they consider good sound by forming most of their tones with the tongue placed as shown in Figure 3.4

FIGURE 3.4

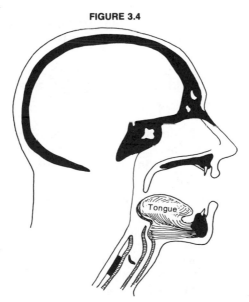

Tongue

Basses are especially prone to think they are producing a rich, mature sound with this tongue position. Considerable effort must be made to get the tongue into the better position shown in Figure 3.5.

FIGURE 3.5

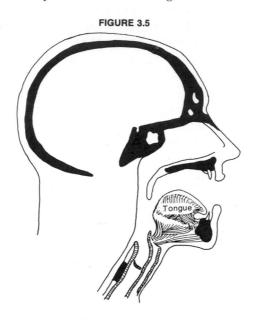

The tongue can be exercised and brought under control. Singers should practice moving the tongue in and out rapidly and turning it over from side to side while keeping the jaw motionless. Working in pairs, singers can check the tongue position of partners while they are singing various vowels. A good vowel for obtaining a correct tongue position is the American $\bar{a}$ as in *day*.

The day_____ in May.

The third factor in the development of resonance is the control of the soft palate. Examine again Figure 3.3. Observe that the soft palate controls the opening from the throat to the nasal cavity. When a person swallows, gags, or regurgitates, the soft palate rises to prevent matter from entering the nasal cavity. The soft palate also rises to close the opening on many consonant sounds. It is apparent that the passage to the nasal cavities must be open if full resonation is to take place. This is especially important for delivery of high tones, which are resonated primarily in the nasal cavities.

The sensation of a lowered soft palate, and thus an open passage to the nasal cavities, is most easily experienced by correctly producing a hum. An affirmative *m-hm,* followed by a sustained *m* or *ng,* will ensure the opening of the passageway. The jaw should be relaxed and well down, the teeth parted, and the lips barely touching. Figures 3.6a and b illustrate correct and incorrect humming placements.

FIGURE 3.6 (a) Teeth apart; lips lightly touching; tongue away from the back of the throat; the soft palate dropped low. (b) Palate up; tongue in wrong position.

CORRECT AND INCORRECT HUMMING PLACEMENTS

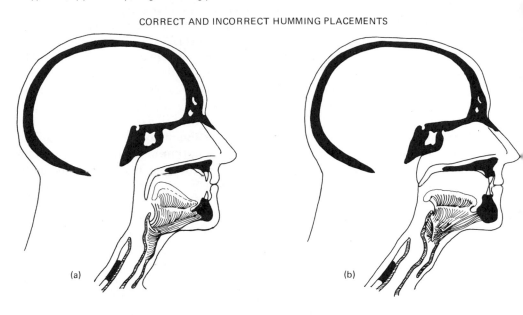

(a)   (b)

Slowly humming down triads [musical notation] will produce the sensation of vibrating, tingling lips, a good sign of free resonation. To create the same sensation of freedom and resonance, repeat this vocalise on $\overline{a}$ *(ay)* or *ä (ah)* with the mouth open wide but covered with one hand. This vocal technique is most valuable for developing choral resonance. Indeed, one of the best things a choir can do to improve its overall sound is to hum properly. Applying the hum to compositions being rehearsed will do much to build resonance into the choir sound.

SPECIAL PROBLEMS OF INDIVIDUAL SECTIONS IN THE CHOIR

Sopranos

When young, sopranos may not have an understanding of breathing, support, freedom, and resonance as outlined in this chapter. With instruction, however, and motivated by the necessity of singing constantly in the upper part of the voice, sopranos usually rapidly develop their vocal capabilities. Because of the strength of their voices, and the fact that they sound the highest, and therefore the most apparent, notes in the ensemble, they often create balance problems. Indeed, sopranos are inclined to over-support and deliver a blast of tone which is sharp in pitch and full of wobble. This section is often the worst in regard to homogeneity of sound.

The training of a soprano section should, from the very outset, be concerned with *flexibility* of production, especially in tone and dynamics. With proper control of the degree of support created, every singer should be able to regulate the tone and dynamic level so they will mesh with those of other vocalists. The key word is flexibility. The human voice is a most glorious musical instrument, capable of delivering an infinite number of pitches, dynamics, and colors appropriate to the full gamut of emotions. It is regrettable that so much vocal instruction is aimed not at developing pliant-ness in the voice but, rather, *rigidity*—an optimum point of sonority or production which the singer employs most of the time. Because of this rather unenlightened pedagogy, sopranos, closely followed by tenors, frequently find it difficult to fit into a choral situation. The conductor will usually find it necessary to train the soprano section to *lighten* its production with some of the exercises found at the end of this chapter (see exercises 51–53). A long, loud, high note, like a home run with the bases loaded, is exciting; constant loud singing, however well produced, is monotonous. Sopranos *must* learn to sing softly, especially on high notes, retaining body and warmth in the tone when they are called for. Without this lightness and variety of color, the traditional soprano-dominated choir is almost an inevitability.

Altos

The alto is the one section of the choir that is rarely called upon to exert itself in high ranges. The part is frequently essayed by sopranos who are timid or lazy. As the section is not often exposed or scrutinized, it becomes a haven for coasters. Unresonated singing from the throat without support is very common in the alto section. The tone is likely to be inactive and flat in pitch, especially between c^1 and g^1.

True alto voices are rare. The choral conductor will usually have to build this section from sopranos who display some heavier quality in their voices. The main problems will be those mentioned above—inactive tone and low pitch due to lack of support.

Altos must also learn to use their *chest voices,* a register sometimes forbidden by voice teachers. Opening these low tones and learning to sing them softly and in tune will do much toward the building of a rich-sounding alto section.

In short, altos must learn to support, to develop an active, focused tone, and to establish an identity which does not sound like weak sopranos who smoke! The alto section should regularly be brought into prominence in rehearsals and built up. The alto and the tenor form the axis of the choral body; neither should be found wanting!

Tenors

The tenor section faces many of the same problems as the soprano; as with the top part, the high male voices tend to protrude through the ensemble. The difficulties are more easily overcome, however, as there are usually fewer tenors, and they seem to be able to control the amount of support more easily. With the ensuing flexibility of tone, tenor voices fit together more easily than soprano.

Tenor voices can tire easily, for they are singing much of the time in the top quarter of their range. They should learn to use their falsetto voices freely, thereby saving their full voice from excessive wear. Moreover, the falsetto tone, clear, light, and free from vibrato, can be a most valuable color to call on in the performance of Renaissance music.

Between the tenor–alto axis, there can be a most valuable borrowing and lending of voices. A high tenor part can be more easily rendered with the addition of a few altos of appropriate quality, and an important alto line can be brought out to almost any degree of prominence desired with some borrowed tenors singing in falsetto or very light head tone. Vocalizing the tenors and altos together in unison in order to unify sound will be found most valuable. Use the exercises at the end of the chapter. Again, I stress the importance of developing flexibility in the vocal production.

Basses

Basses are the foundation of the entire choral structure. Without good bass singers there can be little hope for secure intonation or full sonority. A fine choir can be built with a soprano, alto, or tenor section that is less than magnificent, but a deficient bass section is a most serious matter.

The most common bass problems are weak support resulting in fuzzy pitch; husky tone; a tendency to shout, fade out, or change color drastically on notes above c^1; and sluggishness of articulation resulting in a feeling of lateness in the attack. At the root of all these problems is, once again, the failure to support properly, especially when moving to notes below c. In this range it is easy to sing, as is the case with alto low notes, and basses may coast without supporting. The pitch is then likely to sag, to the detriment of the entire ensemble. A husky tone is usually caused by the tongue obstructing the resonance area. The resultant thick sound undoubtedly sounds better to the singer producing it than to the listener. Basses also must learn to use their falsetto voice, carrying some of its lightness down into the range normally sung by full voice. Once the thinner character of the falsetto has impressed itself upon the ear, basses often find it easier to sing the notes c^1 to f^1 in full voice with a lighter, brighter, more tenor-like sound. Sluggishness of attack is the result of an acoustical phenomenon: low pitches seem to travel slower. Basses, therefore, need to learn to be very alert to entrances, giving a good bite to the tone, *slightly* early in the beat.

It is advantageous to vocalize the soprano and bass together, for these two sections must work closely together. The lower and upper notes of the choir, the diaphony, control the intonation; if they are in tune, the ensemble will be in tune.

SUMMARY

It must be constantly borne in mind that the components of good singing discussed in this chapter are all interrelated and highly dependent on one another. As support is impossible to achieve without good posture, so is resonance dependent upon freedom from tension, a lowered soft palate is brought about by a controlled tongue, and so on. In short, the whole singing mechanism from the balls of the feet to the nasal cavities must function as an integrated unit throughout the entire period that the person is singing. Many choral singers do not understand this point. Granted, the development of this integration requires time and patient effort by the singers and the conductor, but individual growth in singing ability can take place in a well-taught choir if the conductor is convinced of the need and understands vocal pedagogy. Through this work, a choir will begin to move from a commonplace singing group along the path to choral artistry.

Notated below are exercises designed to carry out the vocal techniques outlined in this chapter. They are by no means conclusive and conductors should use them freely as the basis for exercises of their own construction, appropriate to their own particular vocal needs and desires.

VOCAL EXERCISES

For support.

13.

yah	hah	hah	hah	hah
yoh	hoh	hoh	hoh	hoh
yih	hih	hih	hih	hih
yee	he	he	he	he

14.

yah	hah	hah	hah	hah
yoh	hoh	hoh	hoh	hoh
yih	hih	hih	hih	hih
yee	he	he	he	he

15.

yah	ha	ha	ha	ha	ha	ha	ha	hah
yoh	ho	ho	ho	ho	ho	ho	ho	hoh
yee	he	he	he	he	he	he	he	he

16.

yah	ha	ha	ha	ha	ha	ha	ha	hah
yoh	ho	ho	ho	ho	ho	ho	ho	hoh
yee	he	he	he	he	he	he	he	he

17.

yah	ha	ha	ha	ha	ha	ha	ha	yah	ha	ha	ha	hah
yoh	ho	ho	ho	ho	ho	ho	ho	yoh	ho	ho	ho	ho

For relaxation.

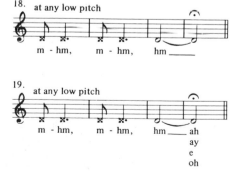

18. at any low pitch

m - hm,   m - hm,   hm _____

19. at any low pitch

m - hm,   m - hm,   hm _____ ah
                                ay
                                e
                                oh

20. at any low pitch

m - hm,   m - hm,   hm ____ ah ____
ay ____
e ____
oh ____

21. at specific pitch

m - hm,   m - hm,   hm ____ ah ____
ay ____
e ____
oh ____

22. at any high pitch

hah ____   hah ____   hah ____
hay ____
he ____
hoh ____

23.

hah ____   hah ____   hah ____   hah ____
hay ____   hay ____
he ____   he ____
hoh ____   hoh ____

For relaxation and resonance.

24a.

hm ____
ng ____

24b.

hm ____
ng ____

24c.

hm ____
ng ____

Also sing 24a, b, and c consecutively

25a.

hm ____
ng ____

25b.

hm ____
ng ____

26.[3]

hm _____
ng _____

Also for intonation.

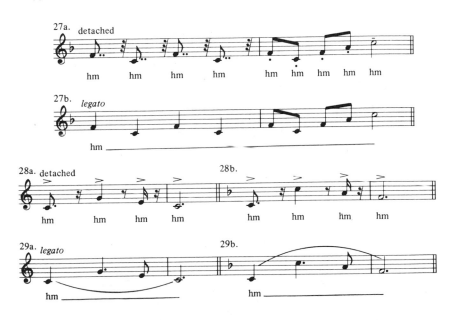

27a. detached

hm   hm   hm   hm   hm hm hm hm hm

27b. *legato*

hm _____

28a. detached   28b.

hm   hm   hm   hm   hm   hm   hm   hm

29a. *legato*   29b.

hm _____   hm _____

For intonation, legato, and to establish primary vowel sounds.

Slowly

30. *legato*

nec	nay	nah	noh	noo	nee	nay	nah	noh	noo	*etc.*
mee	may	mah	moh	moo
tee	tay	tah	toh	too

Also with

noo	noh	nah	nay	nee
moo	moh	mah	may	mee
too	toh	tah	tay	tee

[3]Helga Christensen, *Better Choir Singing* (Dallas: Chorister's Guild, 1973), p. 30.

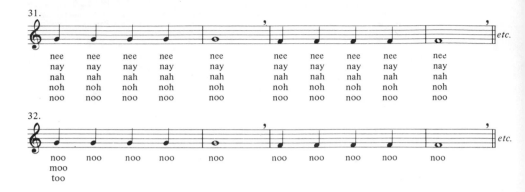

For unification of color.

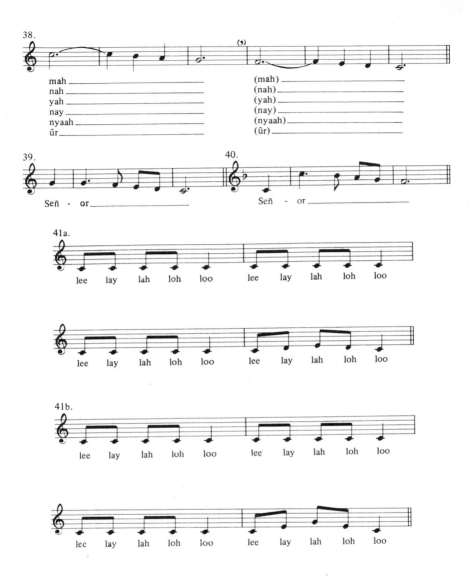

38.

mah _____ (mah) _____
nah _____ (nah) _____
yah _____ (yah) _____
nay _____ (nay) _____
nyaah _____ (nyaah) _____
ûr _____ (ûr) _____

39.   40.

Señ - or _____   Señ - or _____

41a.

lee   lay   lah   loh   loo   lee   lay   lah   loh   loo

lee   lay   lah   loh   loo   lee   lay   lah   loh   loo

41b.

lee   lay   lah   loh   loo   lee   lay   lah   loh   loo

lee   lay   lah   loh   loo   lee   lay   lah   loh   loo

For flexibility.

42a.   42b.
Rapidly

lee   lay   lah   loh   loo   lee   lay   lah   loh   lee   lay   lah   loh   loo
mee   may   mah   moh   moo   mee   may   mah   moh   mee   may   mah   moh   moo
bee   bay   bah   boh   boo   bee   bay   bah   boh   bee   bay   bah   boh   boo
dee   day   dah   doh   doo   dee   day   dah   doh   dee   day   dah   doh   doo

43.

lee	lay	lah	loh	lee	lay	lah	loh	loo	who	who
mee										
bee										
dee										
nee										

44.

| ming - oh | ming - oh | ming - oh | ming - oh | ming - oh |
| ming - ah | | | | |

45.   **46.**

oh - ee	oh - ee	oh	*also*	oh - ee	oh - ee	oh - ee	oh - ee	oh
oo - ee	oo - ee	oo	vee-vee	oo - ee				
oh - ah	oh - ah	oh	mee-mee	oh - ah				
way - oh	way - oh	way	nee-nee	way - oh				
koo - kee	koo - kee	koo		koo - kee				

For extension (not fast).

47.

| mah | mah | mah | mah | *etc.* |
| mah _____ |
| nay | nay | nay | nay | *etc.* |
| nay _____ |
| nyaah _____ |
vee	vee	vee	vee	*etc.*
nee	nee	nee	nee
mee	mee	mee	mee

48.

nyaah _____
nay _____
mah _____

46

For articulation.

49.

la	la	la	la	la	la	*etc.*
ba	ba		*etc.*			
da	da		*etc.*			
lee	lee		*etc.*			
loo	loo		*etc.*			
nyaah	nyaah		*etc.* (difficult)			
nyet	nyet		*etc.* (difficult)			

50. also in inversion

Also with 49 and 50 do physical exercises such as tapping foot, clapping hands,

alternating foot-tap and hand-clap, walk in place (♩), jog in place (♪), swing arms vigorously forward and backward, with partner do kick-swing. (Join both hands with partner. Step on left foot and simultaneously swing right foot across and in front of left foot. Alternate step right and swing left.)

accompaniment to 49 and 50

To lighten top tones—train for high pianissimo.[4]

51.

oh
oo
ûr *(purr)*

To modify high vowels.

52.   53.

oh   ay   oh   ay   oh
oh   ah   oh   ah   oh

For intonation and support.

54.

oo   oo   oo   oo   oo
oh

55.

oo   oo   oo   oo   oo
oh
ah
ay
ee

Combine 54 and 55 various ways—S on 54, A on 55; T on 54, B on 55; S&A on 54, T&B on 55; etc.

56.

te
ay
ah
oh
oo

[4]Christensen, p. 73.

57. Hold a lighted candle as close as possible to the open mouth. Sing *ng*. Observe there is no wavering of the flame. Change the *ng* to *e, ay, ah, oh* or *oo*. Try not to let the flame flicker. This exercise teaches breath control.

58a.

nay___   nay___   nay
nyaah_   nyaah_   nyaah

58b.

nay___   nay___   nay___   nay___   nay
nyaah_   nyaah_   nyaah_   nyaah_   nyaah

59.

bel - la   sên - or   -   a

60a.   60b.

hm_____   hm_____

SUGGESTIONS FOR FURTHER STUDY

For conductors who wish to pursue in greater depth the points covered in this chapter, the following selective readings will provide additional information. In some cases, the reference will present a conflicting opinion.

BOWEN, GEORGE OSCAR, and KENNETH C. MOOK. *Song and Speech*, pp. 3–31, 59–63.
BURGIN, JOHN CARROLL. *Teaching Singing*, pp. 41–59, 80–96.
CHRISTY, VAN A. *Expressive Singing*, Vol. I, pp. 39–58, 81–85.
KLEIN, JOSEPH J., and OLE A. SCHJEIDE. *Singing Technique*, pp. 9–52.
ROSEWALL, RICHARD B. *Handbook of Singing*, pp. 12–35.
VENNARD, WILLIAM. *Singing: The Mechanism and the Technic*, pp. 18–35, 80–122.
WESTERMAN, KENNETH N. *Emergent Voice*, pp. 15–24, 37–44, 73–80.

CHAPTER FOUR
CHORAL TECHNIQUE

When a conductor has prepared in depth for a post of responsibility and has gathered a group of choral enthusiasts who understand and can demonstrate at least some of the vocal techniques outlined in the previous chapter, the teaching-rehearsing procedures begin to move into the area of choral or ensemble technique. The emphasis should now turn from the teaching of individuals to concern for the group as a whole. This is not to say that an individual is to become submerged in the mass; the conductor must never lose touch with the singers as people. However, the singers should now be entrusted to conscientiously apply some of the vocal principles they have learned and to broaden their musical awareness to include the choristers who stand beside them, the entire section in which they sing, and the choir as a whole. As the choir grows in ability, there will always be a need to remind singers of their individual vocal obligations, but the conductor now will give much more attention to the building of a choral instrument or ensemble.

Two factors now deserve careful consideration: the assignment of the individual singer to the proper voice part and the *orderly* seating of the choir. Hasty decisions on these points will cause problems.

ASSIGNING VOICE PARTS

If the choir is an auditioned one, it is relatively easy to determine if a person should sing soprano, alto, tenor, or bass, and whether it should be the first or second part. Range and tone color are the principal factors that determine assignments, the *quality* of the voice probably being more important than the ability to sing certain high or low pitches.

In a less formal situation, such as a volunteer church choir, singers may be reluctant to try out. In fact, an announcement that everyone must have an audition is likely to ensure a much smaller choir, possibly none. Without the audition process, the conductor will have to gain knowledge of the individual voices in the rehearsals themselves. However it is done, the conductor must come to know the vocal capabilities of each choir member and place the singers where their full potential can be realized and *where the choir will benefit most.* Choir members must realize that the needs of the ensemble and the development of its artistry take precedence over the personal desires and ambitions of the singers who comprise it.

The following are qualities you should listen for very carefully when choosing singers for a select ensemble. Overlooking some of these cautions can cause much grief. If you conduct an auditioned choir, take plenty of time at each interview. It is easier to refuse a singer admission than to discharge one later! Be sure you also observe and make note of each singer's walk, stance, attitude, speech, and appearance. These factors will also affect your choir.

Soprano. Listen for a clear sound and the ability to control the amount of vibrato and to sing softly in the upper register. Range:

Those who lack the upper notes, if the quality is right, would still sing soprano, omitting those notes beyond reach. Beware a dark, heavy tone, even if the range is there; a constant, wide vibrato; throat singers; very fast vibrato; opening mouth laterally; and consistent very soft or very loud production. Sopranos of mature years may have lost their control and be beyond repair. They can, albeit reluctantly, make a valuable contribution to the alto section.

Alto. Listen for a warmer, richer sound than that of the soprano. Altos should be able to articulate rapidly and to sing loudly, *in tune,* in the lower register. Range:

Men singing counter-tenor sometimes add great strength to an alto section, but their tone often will not mesh with the female altos. Beware a loud, inactive tone, slightly flat in pitch (indication of lack of support); lateral mouth opening; a consistent mezzo-forte level of production; and sluggish articulation.

Tenor.   Listen for a clear sound with a pleasant vibrato. Seek those with the ability to control dynamic level at any pitch. Range:

Those without the top notes would still sing tenor if the quality is right. Tenors should be able to use falsetto. Beware baritones who think they are tenors but cannot sing above d^1 without going into falsetto; white, lifeless tone, an indication of constant falsetto singing, and mature tenors who can no longer control their vibrato or dynamic level.

Baritone.   Listen for a warm, lyric quality with dynamic control in the upper notes. Range:

Baritones need a keen pitch sense in the lower range; ability to sing from c^1 to f^1 without shouting or going into falsetto; and ability to use falsetto. Beware all notes slightly flat because of lack of support or keen pitch perception; loss of tone between G and c, an indication that the singer may be an undeveloped tenor; "muddy" tone, especially above c^1, due to bad tongue position; and flat pitch below c.

Bass.   This is a rapidly disappearing and endangered species! Listen for ability to sing pitches below G. Range:

Beware inability to sing softly; obscure pitch in low notes; and shouting above f or g.

Most choral conductors must sometimes accept whatever voices are available. Under those conditions, and in educational or other situations, selectivity such as outlined above is not applicable. The singers can be asked to assign themselves temporarily to the voice part of their choice or to consult with the conductor after the rehearsal if unsure as to their voice classification. The conductor must then be willing to work to build up the choir, teaching as well as conducting, and be prepared to move singers to a different section or to different locations within the section, as the voices develop.

SECTIONS

Knowing at least tentatively the voice category of each singer, the conductor now must give attention to the formation of the sections of the choir.

Although some conductors simply ask the basses to sit here, the tenors, there, and so on, we must be aware that considerable variance in sound will occur according to the placement of the singers within the section. Three singers, A, B, and C, may produce quite a different sound when arranged as A – B –C, A –C– B, or B – A – C. Voices that are much alike cancel each other. Dissimilar voices fight. Rate of vibrato and the median dynamic level of production can affect the unification; personality also enters into the situation for some people can adjust more readily than others. No firm rules are available on this activity. Considerable experimentation is usually needed to get the singers in each section arranged so that they are compatible vocally, musically, and socially.

This work requires time, of course, but better results will thereby be obtained than by arranging people by height, putting the insecure singers in the back, stationing the best-looking singers in front of the conductor, or using some of the other unenlightened approaches that are sometimes encountered. Our aim here is to produce a *sectional* sound, completely unified in every way, with neither weak spots nor strong protrusions. The sympathetic singers must be brought together, for this is the first step in developing a choral body that is united in thought, action, and response. Especially in the performance of Renaissance and Baroque music there must be an identifiable, homogeneous, sectional sound. Each genus must work diligently to promote musical and vocal growth within the section. As soon as the section is seated in an optimum arrangement, the singers should be numbered and, insofar as possible, kept in a consistent formation.

Some conductors favor the *section leader* approach, whereby a certain voice becomes a model for the voice part. Fine results are sometimes obtained with this method, but I prefer to think of the section as a whole with all the strong members helping the less secure until one grand concord is established.

Seating the Choir

There are many ways to arrange the various sections to form a choir. Factors to be considered include relative strengths of the different sections, logistics, repertoire, acoustics, and the conductor's choice of sound. In recent years, quartets of singers (SATB) or fully scrambled arrangements (STBSABTS) have been commonly used. Positions such as those in Figure 4.1, which I call "half-scrambles," provide singers with an opportunity for growth in independence while at the same time allowing the conductor to cue each section. These mixed formations are challenging for enthusiastic choristers, help develop good intonation, and are very effective with homophonic literature. Under some conditions, however, the less secure singers will timidly withdraw, causing the stronger voices to protrude through the ensemble fabric. Mixed formations are often less than satisfac-

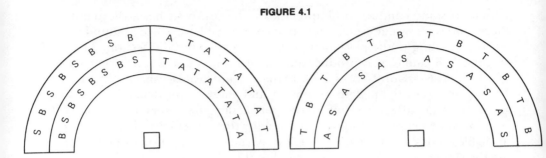

FIGURE 4.1

tory in contrapuntal music, for audiences are unable to follow visually the progression of thematic material, fugue subjects, and so on from one section of the choir to another. However, the growing conductor should certainly experiment with these formations for there are many benefits to be derived from them.

If the decision is made to form a choir with the traditional four sections, and if there is approximately equal strength among the voice parts, the formation in Figure 4.2 is most satisfactory. Here the diaphony (SB) and the axis (TA) can work well together. If the parts are divided, the second part would be behind the first.

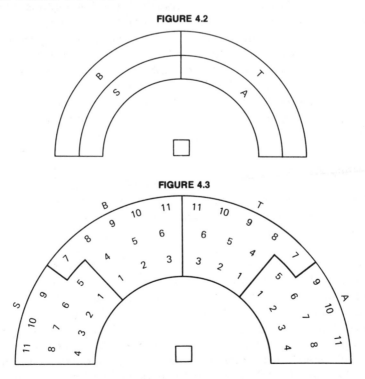

FIGURE 4.2

FIGURE 4.3

Recently, I have come to favor the formation shown in Figure 4.3. With all voice parts in all rows, there is excellent choir unification, yet each section is intact. Each row can be called upon to perform alone for the other rows; the soprano and bass can clearly hear each other and the tenor and alto can assist each other when reinforcement is desired. If one section is short in number, more singers from that section can come into the front row, thereby helping the balance problem.

In extreme cases of imbalanced numbers, a reasonable sound can still be achieved as illustrated in Figure 4.4.

I have already mentioned the numbering of the singers in each section as shown in Figures 4.3 and 4.4. This system is a great convenience at times, for the conductor can call upon different groups to perform, such as S: 1, 3, and 5; or S, A, T, and B: 2, 3, and 4, and so on. The higher voices should have the lowest numbers in each section, so when a divided part is required, the conductor can simply request, "Basses 1 to 3 top part, 4 to 7 lower part" or "Tenors 1 to 5 sing lower part, altos 1 to 4, sing top tenor part." Numbering the singers is a great time-saving technique.

With the choir organized and arranged in a formation appropriate to the composition being rehearsed, the master conductor now begins to move through the rehearsal procedures described in Chapter 1. The process may seem to be complex, but there are actually five distinct, clearly definable technical areas of instruction. The conductor's first goal is to convert the printed page of music into correct sound. In clarifying this sound, the conductor employs choral techniques to act upon the *pitch,* the *rhythm,* the *tone,* the *dynamics,* and the *text.* These choral techniques are greatly dependent upon the vocal techniques discussed in Chapter 2. They are all interrelated and are of equal importance. A fine choir will master these five techniques and apply them to the rehearsal problems as needed so they will be in perfect balance. We will examine these five techniques individually.

FIGURE 4.4

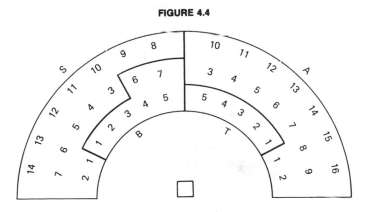

PITCH

A choir must be able to reproduce, with correct intonation, the pitches of the composition as they are notated on the printed page. Until this step is accomplished, no choral excellence can take place. It is at this very basic level of ensemble that countless choirs collapse. I have heard many potentially fine choral ensembles struggling valiantly to give a convincing performance but failing, simply because they did not know the notes or because they sang the notes with such poor intonation that no beauty of tone could ever develop.

The conductor might possibly be blessed with a choir in which most of the members can at once accurately reproduce the pitches called for on the printed pages, without instrumental assistance. Such choirs are rare; more likely there will be a few or only one or two good readers in each section. These readers lead forth with a joyful noise, while the others mumble along creating tone clusters which never completely clear up. Lacking a choir of skilled readers, the conductor must teach the singers the notes: fine choral ensemble cannot take place until all members of the choir can deliver the notes with assurance. Although technique and artistry are closely related, lofty choral experiences can take place only when the notes are learned.

The ability to sing in tune is contingent upon the capacity to listen perceptively, to hear inwardly, and to reproduce accurately a sound transmitted from an external source. As *the basis of all instruction in music is ear training,* the choir must be taught to hear and to discriminate. Indeed, the success of any music ensemble is in direct relationship to this ability. To this end, the following techniques may be helpful:

1. The conductor sings isolated pitches on various vowel sounds and the choir reproduces the sound. This technique may be done in free rhythm with the conductor holding the note while the choir joins in.

2. The first technique can be put into a rhythmic scheme. The conductor should beat time and cue the choir.

3. These exercises can be expanded.

4. The period of silence before the response should be gradually lengthened. The conductor continues to beat.

5. There should be no sound during the rests. The singers should strive to hear inwardly and to respond exactly on the correct pitch without humming up and down to find the note. Never permit your choir singers to hum as a substitute for thinking. The stimulus can gradually be made more complex with longer patterns, wider ranges, dynamic changes, rhythmic variety, and different tone colors. The tonal memory is thereby gradually expanded.

As no printed music is required for these ear training exercises, they can be improvised by the conductor at a technical level appropriate to the ability of the choir. It is important that the singers have a feeling of success when they respond. The maxim, "Take them from where they are," strongly applies. If your choir can remember but two notes a minor third apart, start there, but go on! Use these memory studies for a few minutes in every rehearsal.

6. This technique should also be done using a piano, organ, or other instrument to give the stimulus, with the singers singing back on a neutral syllable—*lah, poo, zee,* or other. Remember to keep an interval of silent thinking between the stimulus and the response.

7. With a stimulus by a keyboard instrument, the singers can be trained to hear very high and very low pitches. Choir members should learn to reproduce any pitch at a comfortable point in their own range.

As the members of the choir are gradually trained to listen more acutely, the conductor will find that use of the traditional Italian syllables for solmization—*do, re, mi, fa, sol, la, ti, do*—will yield considerable benefits. I am not here advocating the singing of all choral music in tonic *sol-fa;* I do, however, urge conductors to use the syllables for the improvement of intonation. For a choir to sing in tune, the performers must be able to reproduce leaps in the melody with absolute accuracy of intonation. Furthermore, working in two parts will give the singers training in singing intervals as well as in listening (and relating) to a second part. These exercises can be started at an early stage; no printed music is necessary for the singers, for the parts are learned by rote from the examples sung by the conductor. The piano should not be used.

In the following intonation studies, the choir should work in two parts—soprano versus alto, tenor versus bass, soprano and alto versus tenor and bass, soprano and tenor in octaves versus alto and bass in octaves, or other combinations the conductor deems desirable in a particular situation. The conductor should sing each part, obtain a response from each group, then call for parts together. The conductor then moves to the next exercise. In all of these studies, extreme accuracy of attack should be stressed. The conductor should beat time constantly and cue the responses. The procedure is outlined below for this example:

Conductor sings and beats time:

do do do

Cues soprano and alto.

S and A sing. Conductor continues to beat time:

do do do

Conductor sings:

do do do

Cues tenor and bass.

T and B sing. Conductor continues to beat time:

do do do

Cues all and calls, "together."

All sing:

do do do

do do do

The following exercises can be carried out in a similar manner; the conductor should construct others suitable to the individual situation. Observe that half-steps are omitted; only the notes of the pentatonic scale (*do, re, mi, sol, la*) are used. Use but a few of these at each rehearsal, but regularly repeat previously learned exercises.

do sol do do do do do sol do do sol mi do sol do

do do do do sol do do mi sol do do do do sol do

As the choir develops accuracy of intonation, half-steps may be introduced. The half-step is an important factor in developing good intonation. It is frequently made too wide.

These two-part studies are based upon principles of music education as set forth by Zoltan Kodaly. It is strongly recommended that choral conductors study his writings and apply his exercises to their own choral situations. Of great value to any choir working to improve its intonation is the set of Kodaly studies titled *Let Us Sing Correctly*.

Rote studies for intonation may also be done in more parts.[1] Proceed as follows:

Everyone learns this bass part in octaves. There must be very clean pitch on both notes. Do not sing rapidly!

Everyone learns this soprano part in octaves. Be sure the reiterated tonic note does not become flat and that the leading tone (E) is high.

[1] These studies are based upon an exercise found in Leonard Van Camp's *Choral Warm-ups for Minds, Ears, and Voices* (New York: Lawson-Gould Music Publishers, Inc., 1972), pp. 3–5. I strongly recommend a careful study of this book.

Now, tenor and bass sing the bass part and soprano and alto sing the soprano part. Work for clean fifths and octaves. Take time to listen. Sustain well.

Everyone learns the alto part in octaves. Keep the leading tone high and guard the tonic!

Now, tenor and bass sing the bass part, soprano and alto sing their own part.

Everyone learns the tenor part. The A *(mi)* must be kept high.

Everyone sings his or her own part. Hold each chord until intonation is perfect.

Also practice in several two- and three-part combinations: S – A, S – B, A – T – B, and so on. Sing on various neutral syllables, *no –loo –paw*. Transpose to other keys. Give the starting chord and have choir members sing silently in their minds, suddenly becoming audible at *. Try *one* person on each part.

The following studies may be taken up in a similar manner.

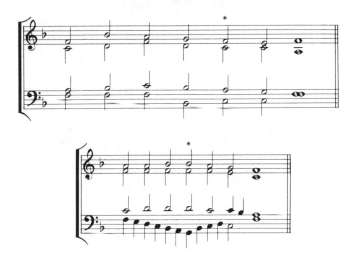

An excellent eight-part intonation exercise is the following:

The second altos sing this note on the vowel OH.

oh

The tone is held to achieve focus and optimum clarity. Breath is taken when necessary by individuals who reenter without disrupting the dynamic level.

The second tenors sing the same pitch. Work to achieve good balance between the two parts.

oh

Add the second bass an octave lower. Attain a perfectly tuned octave and good balance.

oh

Add the second soprano.

oh

Tune and balance. Bring up the dynamic level and try to hear the audible overtone E, the fifth, which sometimes forms in a resonant room when perfect octaves are sounded.

Add the fifth (E), first in the first bass then in the first alto. Balance and tune.

Add the major third (C$^\#$) first in the first tenor, then in the first soprano.

You should now have a perfectly balanced and tuned eight-part chord.

Work with this chord. Make crescendo and diminuendo. Listen to soprano and alto only, tenor and bass only, and other combinations. Use different vowels.

Sing rhythms, such as bee bay bah boh boo   Strive for sonority. You may be making the best sound some of your choir members have ever experienced.

Reading Music

Simultaneously with these studies in intonation, the choir must, of course, begin to study and work with printed music, for this is the major purpose of any choir. It would indeed be difficult to maintain for long the

interest of any group of singers without turning to authentic music literature. Through this study, the ensemble develops as a musical organization.

A vital point in the growth of a choir is its ability to decipher the printed
score—to read the music. Lack of skill in this area can seriously hinder the
advancement of a choral group.

If the choir contains many good readers, its conductor should be most
grateful for being so blessed. However, if the choir, as a whole, *cannot* read, it
is the duty of the conductor to teach the singers enough about the intricacies
of music notation to enable them, with the assistance of a piano or organ, to
bring the printed page into sound. It is not necessary to depend entirely
upon tonic *sol-fa* or other solmization, or upon *ta-fa-ti-fi* or run-run-walk to
achieve correct pitches and rhythms. The following three items may serve as
a starting point for teaching your choir to read.

1. The singers must learn to observe the printed page *keenly*, locating their own
    part, other parts, and the instrumental part (if any), and must learn the
    meaning of the various tempo, dynamic, and expressive indications. Many
    choir singers of long experience have never learned to find anything on the
    page except the text. Your singers are intelligent people. Gradually teach them
    the rudimentary terminology of music notation, and use these terms in re-
    hearsals.
2. Reading music in a choral ensemble is much more a question of *when* to sing
    rather than *what* pitch is to be sounded. Anyone can learn to read simple
    rhythms in a few minutes by counting aloud the beats in a measure while
    following the conductor's pattern. With a reading knowledge of half, quarter,
    and eighth notes, a great deal of choral music can be sung at once. More will be
    said on this subject in the section on rhythm.
3. Consecutive pitches should be recognized as either remaining the same, mov-
    ing up, or moving down; as moving either by step or by skip, and if by skip,
    whether it is small or large. The ear-training exercises in singing thirds, fifths,
    and octaves will be invaluable as singers learn to recognize in print the sounds
    they have previously learned by ear.

Introducing a New Work

With these three basics of music reading in the minds of the singers, the
following procedure may be of help in the introduction and first study of a
new work.

1. After the conductor gives a *brief* orientation to the composition, regarding
    composer, period, style, and text, the rehearsal pianist plays the work through.
    While the pianist plays, the maestro conducts and the singers *silently* follow the
    score. All the singers should have their own music and a pencil for marking
    points of discussion. The pianist, if skilled, may play a combination of accom-
    paniment and voice parts, or may alternate between vocal lines and instrumen-
    tal interludes. Occasionally, two pianists might be utilized, one playing accom-
    paniment and the other, choral parts. This first exposure to the sound of the

composition is very important for the choir and should be carefully worked out by the conductor and the pianist before the rehearsal. The purpose is to give an overall first impression which should be favorable and stimulating.

2. The pianist should again play the work while the director conducts and the choir hums or sings pianissimo on a neutral syllable—*lay, pum, no,* or other sound of the singer's choice. The point of this second step is to permit the singers to try their parts with some assistance from the piano.

3. After a starting chord from the piano, the choir attempts to sing in all parts without instrumental support. The choir should not hum the pitch after receiving the notes from the piano. To do so dulls the ability to listen inwardly. The maestro conducts, cues, and encourages, *but does not sing. The pianist does not play.* An appropriate neutral syllable, selected by the conductor, should be used by all the singers. As any breakdowns occur, the conductor can sing the offending line or ask the pianist to play it. A chord from the piano can then give the pitch to everyone for a restart. It is often beneficial to have the pianist play *two* parts, the one with the problem and a line to support or clarify the passage. *The singers should not sing as the parts are being played.* To do so dulls the inward listening of the singers, encourages a percussive tone in the voices, and creates dependency on the piano for intonation. Play the part first, *then* have the singers respond. In the case of an extremely complex line, it may be helpful to play in octaves or in a different octave from what is notated. The playing of the part should not be loud, percussive, "bangy," or otherwise unmusical.

It is sometimes good to use a different neutral syllable in each of the four parts—soprano on *noo,* alto on *noh,* tenor on *nah,* and bass on *nee.* Putting three parts on *pum* and the fourth part on words is also interesting. You might separate the four parts of the choir into the four corners of the room. Have each section sing while standing in a circle, to facilitate listening to one another. Gradually add the text; this process will be described later in this chapter. It is wise at this stage to hold the dynamic level to an intense, well-supported mezzo-piano. Any louder singing may prevent the singers from hearing each other or themselves. Be very alert to the pitch in the alto and bass; intonation problems often start there.

After two or three successful runs through a composition, section, or passage, the conductor should call for at least a part of it from memory. At a later point in this book we will discuss the importance of being free from the printed page. Many choir singers continue to depend on the printed music long after it has been learned. Rather than singing the music, the singers reread the notes at each repetition. Dependency on the printed page retards artistic growth in choral singing; break away from the printed notes as soon as possible. Sing something from memory at every rehearsal.

Developing Good Intonation

During the initial period of securing the pitches of a composition, care should be taken that the intonation is clean. A choir with poor intonation will have a tone that is dull and lifeless. The following exercises may be helpful in developing accuracy of pitch.

1. Experience good intonation in simple exercises such as those on pages 59–64. Many choirs have never heard what it is like to be in tune.

2. When rehearsing, regularly stop at predetermined points and hold the chord so everyone can listen. Then proceed to the next chord—and listen. Proceed, listen, and so on.

3. As in the exercises on pages 62 and 63, sing silently, inwardly, in the imagination, up to a predetermined point. Then sing aloud. If the chord is in tune, all the singers are thinking good intonation.

4. Learn to sing on the high side of the pitch, *slightly* sharp. Singing even a tiny bit on the flat side, is conducive to the development of dull tone.

5. Sing chords and cause them to go sharp or flat by making a glissando up or down a half-step. For example, sing an E major chord, glissando up to F major, then back to E major, down to E–flat major, back to E major, and so on. Try to create chords in between E major and F major, "in the crack," so to speak.

6. Sing a melody in unison such as the following:

Try to raise or lower the pitch *gradually* so as to arrive in a new key, a half-step up or down, by the end of the line.

7. Sing a simple four-part chorale and, upon a signal from the conductor, raise or lower the pitch during the course of a few notes or a phrase.

8. Practice singing exercises in whole tones.

Whole tone exercises to be done with separate syllable on each note and with long slurs.

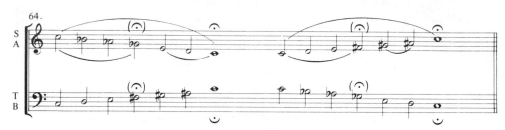

9.   Practice chromatic scale exercises.

Chromatic exercises to be sung with separate syllable on each note and slurred.

T,B octave lower

T,B octave lower

T,B octave lower

69.

10. Carry a pitch pipe or tuning fork with you and try to cultivate the ability to remember specific pitches. Check yourself several times a day.

11. Practice singing intervals both up *and* down from the same tone.

Remember that the most dissonant and non-tonal contemporary music still requires the singer, in most cases, to execute correct intervals.

12. Develop the ability to suddenly sing, without reference to an instrument, a particular chord such as this:

Develop a vocabulary of these "ready in waiting" chords: E^b, $f^\#$, C, D₇, and so on.

There are many reasons why a choir loses the correct intonation. Some of them are as follows:

1. Bad vocal production—poor posture, shallow breathing, lack of support, tension, and failure to resonate. This is the most common cause. Restudy Chapter 3. Bad tone production is the first point to be checked when you are working to correct poor intonation.

2. Insecurity in the size of the intervals to be sung. If the choir does not know the notes thoroughly in a certain passage, especially at the extreme ranges of the voice, the intonation may be poor. Transpose the passage into a comfortable key, possibly up or down a fourth. Have the section sing it until it is perfected, then raise or lower the passage chromatically until the correct key is regained.

3. Tempo too fast or too slow. Rapid tempo does not give much time to find the pitch, and slow tempo may cause the music to lose its forward motion. Adjust the tempo temporarily toward moderato, attain correct intonation, then gradually regain the desired tempo.

4. Dynamics too loud or too soft. Loud singing is very difficult to keep in tune. A choral fortissimo must be gradually built up from a mezzo-forte or forte level

with careful attention being given to vocal technique, especially resonance. Very soft singing can be most beneficial to ensemble development, but once again it must be well supported, free from tension, and active in tone.

5. Wrong concept of the vowel to be sung—*staw* for *star, eny* for *any,* and so on. More will be said on this point later. The choir must be unified on its pronunciation.

6. Incompatible voices singing together. Some voices naturally "fight" when put together, largely because of rate and amplitude of vibrato, or tone color. Restudy the section on seating the choir. The position of the individual singers is a vital point in artistic choral singing. Experiment with different seatings within the section.

7. Fuzziness in the bass section. Any section can, through oversinging or lack of attention, cause the intonation to falter, but if the bass (indeed, the *base)* is solid, the damage will be slight. The bass must always be very clean and clearly audible to all. The ultimate responsibility for good intonation rests with the basses; of course, this does not excuse the other sections from doing their part.

8. A lack of phrase sense. This will cause the pitch to sag. The singers must know when to start and where they are heading. They must move with active tone toward the last note of the phrase, *not losing concentration as they near the end.* Failure to maintain the urgency of the line to the last note of the phrase is a common error in choral singing.

9. Inattention to downward moving passages. Singers often drop their support when the line moves down. All intervals become too large and the pitch rapidly falls. Be sure support is maintained.

10. Inattention to repeated notes. The singers' attention may wander if a single tone is repeated many times. Be sure the original pitch is maintained at each repetition.

11. Inability of the choir members to hear each other. Low ceilings, carpeted floors, acoustical tiles, and wall hangings cut down the resonance of the rehearsal room. Seek active acoustics for your rehearsals and concerts. Experiment with seating as outlined earlier. Too hot or too cold temperatures in the rehearsal room will also adversely affect the acoustical conditions.

12. Disinterest and/or boredom. Inappropriate literature, too much talking by the conductor, or dwelling too long on one point can cause a group to lose interest and pitch simultaneously. Therefore, strive unceasingly to keep the rehearsal active. Move to a new piece. Have the choir stand. Rearrange the seating. Tell a joke. Try to restore the good humor of the choir.

13. Failure to listen and sing inwardly, in the imagination. This is closely related to the previous point. Robert Shaw states, "Mental laziness and sloppy intonation are a pretty smooth couple."[2] Carelessness on this point can be considered "failure to engage the brain before putting the voice in gear."

14. Within a major key, singing flat *mi,* and *la.* Scale steps three and six are often out of tune. Keep these notes and all major thirds high.

15. Failure to attain clean leaps of fourths and fifths. Practice these intervals until they are perfected.

16. Wrong key for a particular acoustical situation. Try transposing up or down a half or whole tone.

---

[2]Harold A. Decker and Julius Herford, eds., *Choral Conducting: A Symposium* (Englewood Cliffs, N.J.: Prentice-Hall, Inc., 1973), p. 35.

17. Inattention to accidentals. Whenever the melodic line or the tonal center is altered by an accidental, the singers must be keenly alert to the harmonic implications created. An accidental frequently causes an unexpected half-step, and great care must be taken in the proper execution of this crucial interval. Very often, the half-step is made too large. Watch for the appearance of new leading tones, *ti* in the key. Leading tones must always be high.

18. Psychological and physiological factors that are beyond anyone's control. Every group, vocal or instrumental, has its days of being out of tune. The human ear, reflecting the general mental and physical condition of the body, can vary amazingly in its acuity. Therefore, when reasonable attention has been given to a period of bad intonation and little improvement is obtained, it is often better to drop the whole matter and wait for a better day. Haranguing the choir on its poor pitch can often make it worse.

Suitability of the Literature

It seems appropriate at this point to mention a vital factor in the development of any choral group—the complexity of the compositions in relation to the technical ability of the choir. Fully as wrong as the conductor who chooses only music simple enough for the singers to learn with tonic *sol-fa*, without instrumental assistance, is the conductor who, bursting with overambition, constantly selects works that are far too difficult for the stage of development of the group at that time. Either approach—literature that is too easy or too difficult—creates an atmosphere in which little growth takes place. If the music is too easy, even if the choir reads it fluently, the ensemble will feel unchallenged and bored. It will be deprived of substantial music which would promote feelings of pride and accomplishment. Once the music has been read, it will be difficult to maintain sufficient enthusiasm to continue rehearsing toward an artistic goal.

More common, however, is the situation in which the compositions under rehearsal are utterly beyond the musical capabilities of the organization. These choirs are characteristically *commanded,* not conducted, by leaders who are motivated by one-upmanship—the junior high school choral teacher who wishes to top the local high school group, or the high school choir that competes with the university choir by spending the entire year struggling to learn Brahms' *Requiem.* In such overly ambitious situations, the notes have to be pounded in, literally, and such a long period passes between the initial exposure to the composition and any feeling of artistic accomplishment, that progression of learning ceases.

Choral rehearsals should constantly include some reading of works not scheduled for public performance. Developing skill in reading new music is one of the best ways to advance a choir. This reading material must be easier than the works scheduled for programs, but must nevertheless challenge the choir in some way, technically or interpretatively.

A distinguishing mark of a successful choral conductor is the ability to determine objectively the technical level of ability of a choir and to select music for study that is within that ability but at the same time advancing it.

RHYTHM

Almost at the same time that the choir is working to read and perfect the pitches of a composition, the ensemble must also deal with various aspects of rhythm. Indeed, the simultaneous solution of pitch and rhythm problems is the foundation of the re-creative process of transforming the printed page of notes into sound. Although for the sake of clarity in this chapter we are considering pitch and rhythm separately, they can scarcely be divided, so closely dependent are they upon one another. Especially notable is the dependency of pitch upon rhythm. Weakness in one or more aspects of rhythm almost always creates havoc with the intonation of a choir.

Within the term rhythm it is possible to define five separate areas for discussion: the *pulse* or beat of the music; *duration* or length of notes and rests; *tempo; meter;* and *phrasing,* the means whereby the musical structure of the composition becomes coherent and intelligible to the listener. There is, in general, a laxity in the use of the term "rhythm," so that it means different things to different people. We will use these five terms to refer to the specific components included within the general area of rhythm.

The Importance of the Pulse

"Concerted music has to be concerted around something, and that something is *pulse,*"[3] says Robert Shaw. The energetic, throbbing heartbeat of music, usually referred to as the *beat,* is possibly the single most important aspect of the art. By means of the pulse, duration of notes and rests is measured, proportion is created, and a sense of inevitabiliy is established in the consciousness of the performer and listener.

The choir conductor must strive to develop in the choir singers an intense feeling for this pulse. The usual physical expressions of pulse such as clapping, tapping, nodding, and so on are but the outward manifestations of an inner, visceral, biological rhythm closely related to the heartbeat and the biological clock. Hand clapping and foot stomping are gut-motivated, to put it another way. Singers must work to recognize and cultivate this *inner sense* of recurrence. Without it, overt actions such as clapping and nodding will be superficial, badly executed, and subject to a multitude of tempo and dynamic fluctuations which destroy the essential feeling of progression to climax. Unfortunately, as there is no way that we can deal directly with this inner motivation, we must attempt to build it up by outward means.

It must be clearly established that the problems of developing a good sense of pulse and duration are not primarily visual or intellectual. The problem is not in *seeing* that there are quarter and eighth notes on the page or

[3]Decker and Herford, p. 38.

in *knowing* that two eighths equal a quarter. The problem is in *feeling* this relationship inwardly before expressing it outwardly in physical motion.[4]

The following exercises will be helpful in sharpening the choir's sense of pulse and duration.

1. As the conductor beats the traditional pattern for $\frac{4}{4}$ with every precise icti, the singers establish a firm pulse in quarter notes with a light hand clap. Hold one hand stationary and clap the four fingers of the other hand upon it. The tempo should be about ♩ = 72–76. A foot motion produced by keeping the ball of the foot on the floor and lifting the heel slightly and dropping it can be added to the hand motion. Work to maintain a precise quarter note pulse in hands and feet without the slightest fluctuation in tempo. The tendency will be to go faster; guard against it. At this point a little game much enjoyed by the young choirs can be played by having the conductor count aloud "one–two–three" and requiring the singers to continue counting silently, inwardly, in the tempo given up to twelve. Precisely at twelve everyone makes a loud hand clap or foot tap. Closing eyes ensures independence of action.

2. Vary this basic rhythm exercise by drilling in $\frac{2}{4}$ and $\frac{3}{4}$. Change the tempo slightly. The conductor beats one measure silently, and the choir begins its hand–foot motion on the downbeat of the second measure and continues in tempo *without the conductor's beat pattern*.

3. Set up the hand–foot motion and let the choir *speak* a precise "one–two–three–four," "one–two," or "one–two–three" in quarter notes.

4. Maintain the hand–foot motion and speak as above with subdivisions: "one and two and" (♩♪ ♩♪), "one–ta–ta two–ta–ta" (♪♪♪ ♪♪♪), or "one–ee–and–uh two–ee–and–uh" (♪♪♪♪ ♪♪♪♪).

5. Create variations on exercise 4 such as the following:

It will be found to be much more difficult to keep the tempo as the rhythm changes from ♪♪♪♪ to ♪♪♪ to ♩♪ .

6. Create speaking exercises in two or three parts, such as

---

[4]This point is elaborated upon in Charles Heffernan, *Teaching Children to Read Music* (New York: Appleton-Century-Crofts, 1967), pp. 14–16.

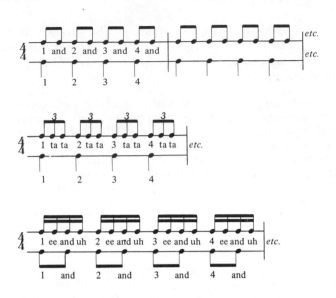

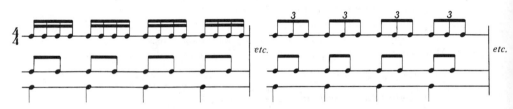

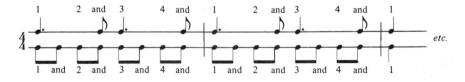

These speaking exercises may be made as simple or complex as the conductor feels is necessary to advance the rhythmic perception of the choir. Be sure the hand–foot pulse in quarter notes is cleanly maintained at all times and that the speaking is very crisp and clean.

As security is gained in holding tempo firmly, dotted rhythms should be introduced as below:

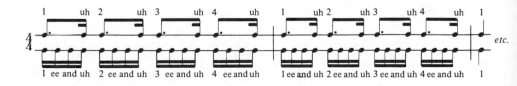

All the preceding exercises should also be practiced with neutral speaking syllables—*tah, dee, pooh,* and so on. Good humor devices are available in quantity here. When these studies are *very secure,* and only then, the hand clap and the foot tap can be eliminated.

Reading Rhythm Patterns—Duration

As rapidly as possible the choir should learn to read rhythmic notation. The point has been made that success in reading music is highly dependent upon extreme accuracy in rhythm; if the singer knows exactly *when* to sing, the careful observation of the altitude of the note will usually guide the voice to the correct pitch. If, on the other hand, there is rhythmic insecurity, no confident forward motion can develop. It is, therefore, very worthwhile to spend time reading only the rhythm of the composition being rehearsed.

If the sense of pulse has been well founded in the choir, as put forth in the preceding exercises, the next step is to teach duration or time value of notes. With an explanation of ♩, ♫, and 𝅗𝅥, the conductor can either construct some simple reading exercises or turn at once to easy printed music. Two important points must be established: (1) the singers must know how many beats there are in each measure and precisely at what point each beat falls *within* the measure; (2) the singers must recognize the value of the notes and rests and be able to set them onto the correct beat.

To accomplish these points, try the following:

1. Let the choir members all beat time together, each using the traditional conducting patterns shown in Figure 4.5, at the same time counting aloud the beats, "one–two–three," and so on.

FIGURE 4.5

2. Have the choir read simple exercises from a chart or single lines from easy printed music, maintaining the conducting pattern and counting the rhythm aloud.

75

The singer is therefore required to know what beat within the measure is being sounded. It has long astonished me that many (most?) singers do not count *at all,* but keep their place by watching other parts, taking cues from the conductor, following the words, guessing, hoping, and so on. They become lost when tied notes, syncopations, or rests are encountered. By being required to count, they are forced to read. By conducting themselves, they are more easily able to keep their place and to feel the meter. In watching the choir conduct the patterns, the maestro can determine if the singers really do know where they are in the measure.

Rests should be performed with great precision. They are vital to the line in which they occur and must be felt with great intensity. Singers must be made aware that rests are not "time-outs" or periods of repose but, rather, *precise blocks of silence* during which one must prepare for the next tones to be sounded at exactly the correct moment. Singers must learn to remain actively involved during rests.

In the counting technique expounded here, rests are indicated by a cessation in the audible counting. The conducting pattern, of course, continues unabated.

Tied notes and syncopations may be added to these exercises. The following study will serve as a guide for most rhythmic complexities that will be encountered.

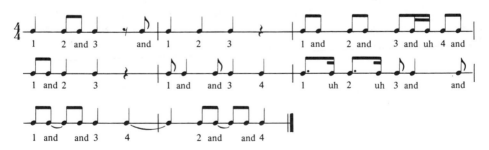

Breaking Down the Beat

To create a greater feeling of continuity or flow in the line and to experience more easily a feeling of sostenuto in long notes, it is valuable to select a basic flow of eighth or sixteenth notes, or some other pattern, such as ♩ ♫ and break down the entire line into these note values, using the principles outlined above. Precision in the execution of longer note values cannot be attained without a feeling for the underlying subdivision. Work to develop your singers' skill in relating to an eighth or sixteenth note basis. The need for competency in this technique cannot be overemphasized.

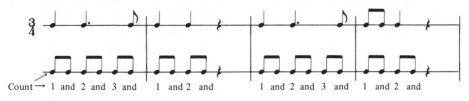

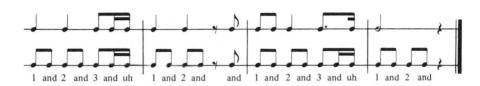

Often, when a choir has difficulty getting a strong sense of forward motion into a melodic line, a greater feeling of progression can be created by breaking the melody down as follows:

Broken down:

or:

Sing first using the numbers and subdivisions, then change to a softly reiterated vowel, such as *loo, noo,* or *noh.* In this way, a strong legato will be combined with the already precise rhythm.

It is also interesting to do four-part clapping and stamping together with a spoken breakdown of the beat. Having begun to speak a precise one and two and three and four and one, and so on in a composition in $\frac{4}{4}$, the singers then clap the rhythmic pattern of their own part, continuing to speak the breakdown. Additional interest can be created by obtaining different tones in the rhythmic claps—sopranos make a light hand clap, altos clap with cupped hands, tenors slap hand on upper leg, and basses tap their heel. A choir that can do this exercise, especially in countrapuntal music, knows when to sing its notes.

It is apparent that work with rhythmic techniques such as those above will produce considerable accuracy in the duration of notes and rests. The sense of pulse should also improve during this study. A choir that gains facility in these techniques will move more confidently into new repertoire; less time will need to be spent in drilling out the individual parts. In fact, a very good first reading of a composition would be to work with rhythm only. This step might be taken before the choir hears the composition played through as in the procedure outlined in the section on Introducing a New Work. Persistent effort in reading rhythm will yield great benefits to any choir.

Strengthening the Rhythmic Aspects

As the singers gain confidence with a composition, two techniques may be helpful in securing additional rhythmic accuracy. One is to sing on neutral syllables; a most beneficial sound to use is *pum.* The syllable should be sung at mezzo-piano level and should be executed with a loose jaw in a rapid down-up motion. The open vowel sound should be made as short as possible, the *um* being sounded immediately after the *p.* The singers should strive for good resonance and make a slight crescendo on each *um.* Have them sing the composition using a separate *pum* on each note, which will then be strongly accented. This technique brings the moving parts into prominence, enabling them to be heard by all the singers. The constantly sounding *m* builds resonance and an improved tone will be heard almost at once. Two cautions with the use of *pum:* (1) firm support must be maintained by all the singers; otherwise the pitch will fall because of the dark color; (2) *pum* is most valuable in the lower and middle ranges of the voice—its use on high passages causes pinching and loss of flexibility.

A second valuable technique to increase rhythmic awareness is to sing every note in a composition as if it were a sixteenth note, or as short as possible. Do not sustain any note.

This technique not only requires extreme accuracy in sensing the exact moment of attack on each note but also calls for rapid, keen pitch perception since there is only an instant to find the center of the pitch. The vowel to be used depends somewhat on the skill and experience of the singers in finding pitches rapidly. The brighter vowels of *dee* or *tee* are easiest; *lah* or *law* are good and, in addition, provide tongue exercise. *Doo* or *too* produce a lovely Baroque-organ-like tone which is a delight to hear. Once again, this technique is most beneficial at soft dynamic levels in the lower and middle ranges. It can become devastatingly out of tune if used by a choir weak in vocal technique; under those conditions it is damaging rather than beneficial. Either sing it in tune or not at all.

All of these exercises have had, as one of their aims, the securing of the inner sensation of regularly recurring pulse. There cannot be too much attention given to this all-important element of music. The pulse governs the forward motion, and without this motion the music is lifeless.

The Speed of the Beat—Tempo

It is, of course, possible for the speed of the pulse to vary. Ritards and accelerandos are two of the ways in which expression is developed in music. Yet it seems to me that the most important thing about tempo, for that is what we are discussing here, is the ability of the choir to *maintain* a tempo once it has been set. Indeed, one of a conductor's primary responsibilities is to establish the correct tempo, but once it is given, the group must unfailingly hold it until an adjustment is called for. A choir that lags behind or rushes forward is no joy to conduct or hear. Conductors who are constantly stamping their feet, clapping their hands, snapping their fingers, or shouting "Look at me," in order to control the tempo, must do additional teaching and explaining as they hone the singers' sense of inner pulse.

Rushing and lagging are largely the result of inattention or loss of concentration on the pulse, due to certain distractions. In particular, rushing is almost always due to reiterated rhythmic patterns. It is very difficult to maintain the tempo when the music calls for long passages of ♩ ♫♩ ♫ or ♩. ♫.♩. Even passages of ♩ ♫♩ ♩ are very likely to be rushed, and the conductor must be extremely alert to catch this problem. Lagging, a much more common problem than rushing, may be caused by insecurity in pitches or by failure to sense the subdivision within the longer note values. A slow or moderate melody in quarter notes cannot be kept in strict tempo without a keen awareness of the eighth or sixteenth note basis. The exercises on page 77 should assist in overcoming this tendency.

Another reason choirs lag or at least do not move the music forward is because they put too much emphasis on the downbeat of the measure. It is often the conductor's fault that this happens. In an enthusiasm and desire to instill excitement into the singers, he or she may overconduct, putting too much emphasis on the strong beats of the pattern with the result that the music becomes "hung up" on the first beat of each measure. The music slowly dies of strangulation.

In order to be expressive, music must always achieve a disciplined freedom from restraint, a kind of controlled abandon, or buoyancy. We shall discuss this freedom of movement in Chapter 5, but for the present it suffices to say that the choir, in working with the basic rhythmic techniques given above, must constantly seek independence, lift, and freedom from heaviness at every point in the measure or line. One of the first ways to begin to develop this sense is for the conductor to exert less control over the ensemble—and occasionally to stop conducting. This act is an acid test of the conductor's confidence in the group, of how well the singers have been taught, and of how secure they are in the rhythm. So long as the choir depends on the conductor to maintain the tempo, this freedom or buoyancy cannot develop.

Such a move toward independence is exactly the opposite approach to that taken by charismatic conductors who assemble a group of singers merely to produce a concert. Under those conditions little is done beyond correcting mistakes. There is no analysis of problems or building of technique and musicality. Teaching by imitation leads nowhere. Performances for the enjoyment and edification of others are important to any ensemble, but rehearsals must produce training that lasts far beyond the particular event under preparation. The great conductors are all teachers of their forces, not just sergeants of notes and pieces.

It would be well at this point to review all the exercises in rhythm and see to what extent the choir can carry them on without the conductor, once they have been set in motion.

Meter, together with its effect upon phrasing, is a vital component of choral artistry. We shall examine it in depth in Chapter 5.

TONE

The first thing to which an audience reacts at a choral concert, with the exception of the visual aspects, is the *tone* made by the choir. The listeners' attention is at once drawn to the quality of sound being delivered—its richness, maturity, fullness, and clarity—also, in many cases, to the lack of any of those characteristics. From that moment when the first chord is sounded, and throughout the entire concert, the tone of the choir is a highly conspicuous part of the total presentation. The repertoire may be varied and worthwhile; the compositions may be performed with good intonation and rhythm and with an air of confidence and sincerity. However, if the tone is unpleasant, weak, thin, harsh, monotonous, or inappropriate to the particular work being sung, the reaction of the audience will not be favorable. It may startle some conductors to realize that the most apparent result of their work with a choir is likely to be the tone. Within a relatively short time after a conductor takes over a choir, it will have a sound of its own, and this sound is the result of what the conductor does or does not do with the tone. Conductors' concepts of choral tone are developed by their listening experiences and by their experimentation.

Choral conductors vary amazingly in their attitude toward tone. Some choirs are carefully trained year after year to consistently produce a particular tone which has become traditional with that group. The tone might be described variously as cool, hooty, pure, white, warm, deep, throaty, covered, or even boring. At any rate, the tone is the important thing with that particular choir, and all the other components of choral music assume a secondary position. It has been said of certain conductors that they would gladly conduct a choir in a C major chord all day long if only the right tone could be produced!

At the other end of the scale of attitudes toward tone are those conductors who never mention the subject! Often, the primary concern of these conductors is the repertoire; once the notes are in decent order, they move on to other works. The tone that their choir delivers varies greatly from season to season and is entirely dependent upon the vocal characteristics and abilities of its members at any particular time. One year, the choir may have a group of mature contraltos; the next, in the same section, merely old and tired sopranos. Helden tenors or converted baritones assisted by women singing in chest voice, to this conductor it makes no difference—the music's the thing!

Somewhere between these two extremes are the conductors who occasionally bring up the subject, often confusing tone with dynamic level. There are, fortunately, enlightened conductors who perceive tone as something stylistically inherent in a particular composition and earnestly try to produce a tone that is appropriate to a certain work or even section of a work. The tone is varied according to the changing needs of the repertoire. Robert Shaw terms this approach a seeking for *dramatic integrity* in the tone.

Many factors contribute to the kind of sound a choral group will produce. First, there is the intrinsic tone of the group as determined by its membership. Opera choruses comprised of soloists, junior high school girls' choirs, and volunteer church choirs in senior citizens' retirement centers all have characteristic sounds. Too many choral directors merely accept, with an air of resignation, the inherent tone of their ensemble. Unaware that this sound can be altered, they patiently or impatiently await a change of membership.

Realistically speaking, it is quite obvious that no amount of work can make the teenage girls' choir sound like the opera chorus, but *any* choir can vary its sound somewhat, frequently to an amazing extent. The determining factor is the vocal technique of the individual singers. Conductors must work for *flexibility* of production; they are, therefore, occasionally at variance with some voice teachers who seek to find in their pupils the point of maximum resonation and then focus all their attention on that sound. This approach produces *rigidity* of production and trains singers who dislike singing in choirs and, indeed, have little to contribute to a sensitive ensemble.

Let us now consider some of the techniques by which the conductor can vary the tone of the choir. Choral tone is influenced by several clearly defined areas: vocal production, pitch, dynamics, and vowels. As with practically all the choral techniques under consideration in this book, control of tone quality is basically dependent upon vocal technique. Until the members of the choir are secure in their demonstration of posture, breathing, and support, and until they can sing without tension, resonating properly, little can be done to produce variations in tone color. This is why untrained or inexperienced choirs are boring to hear; lacking vocal technique, they can produce but little variation in their sound. The conductor must constantly keep in mind the need for good vocal production as set forth in Chapter 3.

Active Tone

A well produced vocal tone must also be *activated*. All choral sounds, regardless of their dynamic level and color, must have a sense of vitality and direction—an intensity, a vigor, a feeling of energy. This strength of character can be developed in the choir by examples of the word *go* sung by the conductor. Sing the word on a medium pitch, without a sense of command or conviction; then sing the word with authority and assurance. Ask the choir to imitate in both cases. The preference for the second example should be clear. An excellent example of the singing of this word with overwhelming conviction occurs at the end of Act II of Wagner's *Die Walküre*. Wotan tells Hunding to return to Fricka. The two words *"Geh! Geh!"* although sung at a low dynamic level, are delivered with such intensity that Hunding falls dead to the ground! Study that model.

The choir might then sing a chord on *go*.

Try to develop a tone of absolute authority and total command regardless of the dynamic level. Stress the importance of a mental concept of power *before* sounding the chord. The single word becomes a complete statement, a kind of one-note phrase. Insist upon inner conviction until the chord says everything possible.

Having achieved some success in singing a convincing verb *go,* the choir might turn to a composition under rehearsal and select some key words for this one-note phrase treatment. Verbs such as *sleep, rest, sing, call, shout* and nouns such as *child, beast, friend,* and so on, will give the singers experience in forming strong mental concepts which affect the tone. A sensitive choir must indeed learn to paint the key words of a composition with an appropriate, active tone color. Monochromatic singing is deadly to listen to.

Move next to a two-note phrase, first with separate words *go! go!* then with a single slurred word. Ascertain that the tone remains *active* at all times.

Continue this exercise through three-, four-, and five-note phrases until the choir senses the need for constant *active* tone. Other verbs such as *come, sleep, sing,* and so on, can be used. Then move to nouns and adjectives, always striving for *conviction.* This development of active tone is very important. Always work to sing *through* the entire phrase with unabating energy to the *last instant* of tone.

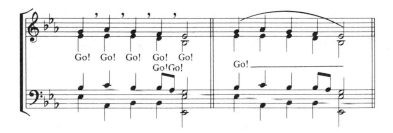

Articulation

The singers must be able to articulate in at least three different ways: *marcato, staccato,* and *legato.* The studies in staccato in Chapter 2 will have prepared the singers to perform with crisp rendition of very short notes. Actually, in staccato, the listener's ear is drawn toward the spaces *between* the notes. The studies on *pum* and other short syllables, outlined on page 78, will further assist in developing clean staccato articulation.

In marcato, each *note* is given emphasis and is slightly separated from adjacent notes. Each note has a feeling of completeness; the studies above on *go* will have prepared the singers for this concept. Marcato is a valuable articulation in choral music, for with it, emphasis can be brought into sustained lines which might otherwise be wearisome. Marcato must be used sparingly, however. The ear quickly tires of a long series of accented notes.

At the core of a great choir's technique is its ability to sing legato. Skill in singing a series of notes with no diminution of continuity between the notes is required in most of the great choral literature. The slurred exercises on *go*, given above, will have provided models of legato, as will have many of the vocal technique studies. Developing a powerful sense of legato, of connection from note to note, may be further assisted by this exercise.

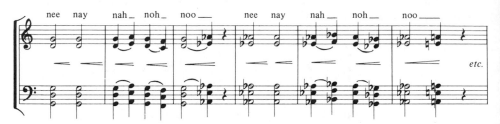

The satisfactory rendition of this study, with its powerful forward thrust, is dependent upon the execution of a controlled mini-crescendo on each half note or pair of slurred quarter notes. Manipulation of subtle changes in dynamics is an important part of legato.

Tone Color

Once the singers have developed control of their voices in articulating an active tone, they should consider the technique of altering the color of the sound. This concept is probably best approached by means of a vowel chart as in Figure 4.6.

The choir should sing a well-produced chord on an *ē* vowel; use a word such as *see*. Work to get a sensation of the tone being resonated as far forward in the nasal cavities as possible. Try to get a strong feeling of nasality into the tone, then refine out the unpleasantness. Take the chord up and down chromatically and sing at different dynamic levels. Try to retain at all times the same tone quality, which should be very bright and penetrating. Turn then to a simple composition already learned and sing it entirely on the *ē* sounds; use a consonant before the vowel to help reset the tone at each note. Experiment using a separate word *fee, mee, nee, tee, dee, pee,* and so on, with each note. Activate the tone and do not sing too loudly. Maintain and refine the bright sound. Now sing the text of the composition, and try to inflect all

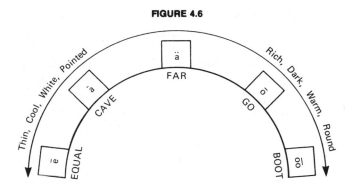

FIGURE 4.6

the vowels with a bit of the ē sound. It should be rather easy to keep everything bright, for the tonal concept will have already been established in the ears of the singers.

Now try the same procedure using an o̅o̅ vowel. Strive for a dark, warm tone which feels resonated far back in the throat. Vary the pitch and dynamic level. Apply the o̅o̅ sound to the same composition as with ē and try to retain the dark sound. Sing the text, and round every vowel to make it feel like o̅o̅.

With these experiments, the following results will become apparent:

1. Although ē produces a pointed sound and o̅o̅ a round sound, different singers have varying degrees of success in producing point or roundness. Success is partly due to vocal control or technique, but individual voices have a natural tendency toward light or dark color. Some are mixed. It would therefore be difficult to produce a dark-toned choir from all light voices, and vice versa. Mixed voices provide the greatest flexibility.
2. Individual voices stand out more on ē. They mesh better with o̅o̅.
3. The o̅o̅ sound is difficult to keep in tune.
4. Either vowel is difficult to sing at high pitches.
5. Both vowels are tiring to sing for an extended period.
6. While ē and o̅o̅ represent the perimeters of choral color, *any* vowel can be inflected to some extent toward either the light or dark side.
7. In seeking a sound that is pleasant to hear, the higher one goes in pitch the *rounder* one sings; lower pitches come through better if the sound is *pointed*.
8. The rate and amplitude of the singer's vibrato affect the vowel production. An o̅o̅ with a straight tone contains little warmth. Choir singers must, therefore, be willing and able to control their vibrato.

Further experiments can be carried on by using the vowel chart in Figure 4.6. It is often valuable to vocalize the choir on descending and ascending scales and exercises and then apply the vowel sounds to compositions. The vowel $\bar{a}$ *(cave, day)* lends itself to a great deal of interesting experimenting, for the vowel can be inflected with either biting nasality or roundness. When refined, $\bar{a}$ can give great brilliance and resonance to the tone; when rounded and sung softly, it still has keen intensity and emphasis. The vowel $\ddot{a}$ *(far)* lies almost exactly at the midpoint between the extremes of light and dark tones we have mentioned and can be inflected in either direction. $\bar{O}$ *(go)* is inherently quite dark and is difficult to brighten. The full vowel chart (Figure 4.8, p. 96) can provide additional experience in the development of light and dark tone. The dark vowels are the more difficult to develop; it requires great concentration to avoid going flat. When well under control, however, the dark vowels can produce a beautiful choral sound; many conductors favor them.

Light and dark tone may be contrasted as follows:

LIGHT TONE. *Advantages:* has brilliance and great carrying power, is exciting, objective, good for tuning, very clear. *Disadvantages:* is difficult to blend, can be harsh, lacks personality.

DARK TONE. *Advantages:* is easy to blend, has sensuous sound, is personal. *Disadvantages:* is difficult to tune, lacks clarity, lacks power.

By no means do I advocate training a choir to sing always with the same tone. In spite of those well-known groups who are revered for their light or dark tone, the one-color approach is essentially wrong in that, unless the choir sings only from a limited period of music literature, the one chosen color will be inappropriate for at least half the repertoire being performed.

It is true, however, that developing an ensemble that can vary its tone substantially from one composition to another is a most difficult task. It can hardly be done at all with choirs of young voices. Significant changes can be obtained only with substantial growth in vocal technique. Thus comes the need to teach voice production constantly in rehearsals.

The preliminary exercises in this chapter are presented to give the conductor and the singers experience with different kinds of tone. If the concept of variation of tone is instilled right from the start, it will be easier at a later time to find the appropriate color for a particular passage, movement, or composition. These exercises, therefore, are *techniques* of tonal variation—the manipulation of the overtones to produce certain colors— and are not to be confused with *motivation* of tone.

Finding the appropriate tone for a certain piece of music is another matter. The whole subject is open to considerable controversy and will be an important part of the next chapter. At this point in our development of an expressive choral instrument, it is sufficient to ask that conductors be aware of the absolute necessity for variety of tone color, and that they have in their ears a clear concept of a sound that is personally satisfying and within the technical grasp of the singers.

DYNAMICS

Of the various components that a musical performer calls upon to produce expressivity, variation of the dynamic level (loudness and softness, if you will) is the factor most frequently employed. In contrast to rubato or other rhythmic subtleties, or to variations in tone quality, changing the dynamic level of an ensemble is a relatively simple matter. The conductor simply asks for, or indicates with an appropriate gesture, "louder" or "softer."

Yet, in spite of the ease with which a choir can change its dynamic level, it is always amazing to me to hear so many choirs that have good pitch, rhythmic control, and a pleasant tone, yet produce boring performances because of little or no variation in the dynamics. With the exception of special points in the composition, a choir, unless well taught, will deliver most of its tones at the level of mezzo-forte, a dynamic Koussevitsky abhorred as "di most baddest nuance *qui existe.*"[5] Indeed, mezzo-forte and forte seem to be the only two levels of dynamics familiar to many choirs. They will gladly attempt a fortissimo, usually with raucous results, but suggestions from the conductor that it would be nice to sing more softly are often met with the downcast faces of singers who have lost the joy of life. Attempts to sing mezzo-piano or piano are characterized by a dispirited, lifeless tone which, as soon as the conductor's back is turned, figuratively speaking, at once returns to mezzo-forte. A choral pianissimo, one of the most sublime sounds in all music, is outside the experience of most choirs.

As was the case with tone, dynamics are influenced by several intrinsic factors. Conductors should be aware of these facts:

1. The voices of different singers have different degrees of loudness as the median point for speaking or singing.
2. The ability to change the dynamic level of one's speaking or singing varies greatly with the individual.
3. Vocal technique, once again, is the principal factor in controlling the dynamic level.
4. Vocal instruction is frequently directed only toward *increasing* the size or dynamic level of the voice. Quiet vocalises may be neglected.
5. Pitch level is likely to be associated with dynamic level: high with loud, low with soft. People love long, loud, high notes!

Every choir should have available six levels of loudness which can be called upon to express the requirements of various musical climaxes. These six levels should be made familiar to the choir by means of a simple chart as below and then experienced in exercises.

[5] Harry Ellis Dickson, *Gentlemen, More Dolce Please!* (Boston: Beacon Press, 1969). p. 47.

6	*ff*	fortissimo	extremely powerful, overwhelming, should be rarely used
5	*f*	forte	loud, strong, full, emphatic
4	*mf*	mezzo-forte	rather loud, like animated conversation, bland, use rarely
3	*mp*	mezzo-piano	conversational, little emphasis, a good rehearsal level, clear
2	*p*	piano	very quiet, must have body, draws attention
1	*pp*	pianissimo	barely audible, very light (soft), a stunning dynamic

If a choir has such a chart for reference, each of the six dynamic levels will become a meaningful specific rather than a relative matter. The conductor sensing a need for forte or piano need but call for that level. To achieve this understanding, it is suggested that the singers work first for a clearly defined forte (level 5) and piano (level 2) in simple chords and exercises.

Obtaining the forte will be easy, but it must be well supported and resonated with freedom. There must be no feeling of strain, harshness, or distortion. The tone must be confident and commanding. After the concept is well established, the conductor should select a very simple, short composition and have it sung forte throughout. Beware that high notes are not constantly loud and low notes soft, an infallible sign of lack of dynamic awareness. Do not let the general dynamic level rise to fortissimo, and, above all, do not let the intensity lag to where the level is no longer forte but mezzo-forte, lacking in conviction, strength, and emphasis. Singing forte for any length of time is very difficult: it is tiring. Therefore, singers are likely to give up part of their support and concentration and fall back to the bland mezzo-forte level.

A stirring forte delivered with a good tone can provide thrilling moments in a performance. At these points, the audience participates vicariously in the tremendous expenditure of energy displayed by the performer and finds the experience exciting. The release of power, as in athletic events, is a vital element in a good performance of music.

A proper sounding piano level can be developed best directly out of a forte. Have the chorus sing the chord and/or the exercise above *forte,* and check that vocal production is as fine as can be obtained. Then, without permitting any relaxation in posture or support, have them sing the same chord or exercise *piano.* Work for vitality and body in the soft sound. Alternate between loud and soft. At that point it should become apparent that loudness is essentially dependent upon the amount of air passed through the vocal cords. The components of good vocal production— posture, support, breathing, freedom from tension, and resonation—must remain more or less constant in spite of the dynamic level. Considerable practice may be required before this point is fully appreciated.

A secure understanding and feeling for true forte and piano should be developed before other dynamic levels are attempted. Mezzo-piano will be found to be a very useful dynamic level for the rehearsal of pitches and rhythms. If produced with fullness, it is appropriate for the performance of a great deal of choral music, especially that of the Renaissance. Mezzo-piano encourages blend of the various voices and clarity in the lines. It is less wearisome for the audience to listen to for an extended period than mezzo-forte. When a choir has mezzo-piano as its midrange dynamic, there are still available sufficient louder levels which can be used for emphasis. Yet, these louder levels of mezzo-forte and forte can be freely produced without harshness and with good tone. If, however, the choir is operating most of the time at mezzo-forte, it will be necessary to go to fortissimo to secure the same degree of contrast that is obtained between mezzo-piano and forte.

Training a choir to sing freely with a good tone at the softer dynamic levels is not easy. It requires persistent effort by the conductor, who must often do battle with singers who claim they cannot sing softly or that singing softly ruins their voices. Both these claims are untrue. People who cannot sing softly are lacking in vocal technique; they can be taught as explained in Chapter 3. As to the second claim, I can truthfully say I have never, in thirty years of working with singers, known any performers who harmed their voices by singing softly, and I *have* known many who have severely damaged their voices by constant loud singing.

One of the most beautiful aspects of choral music is singing at the quieter dynamic levels. The conductor must work to open up these areas to the choir. Choral music is, on the whole, performed at lower levels of dynamics than instrumental music. Band and orchestra conductors who come to work with choral groups often expect the singers to produce high levels of sound more or less constantly. Harshness of tone and damage to young voices sometimes result from this approach to singing. The vocal production of the singers must be so well secured that a full range of dynamics is possible. Being able to select a particular dynamic, loud *or* soft, and to maintain it, is the first step in controlling the dynamics in a composition.

Even more important to artistic choral singing is the ability to effect subtle nuances of loud and soft as required by crescendo and diminuendo. Actually, ━━━━ and ━━━━ are the most frequently used devices for expression in music. Subtle crescendo and diminuendo are a vital part of phrasing, without which cohesion in the musical ideas cannot be established.

Singers seem to be able to control crescendo better than diminuendo. As the ━━━━ is attempted, too much breath will be used. The

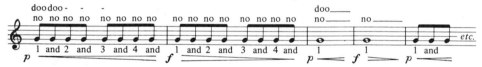

━━━━ then collapses because of lack of support.

A *controlled* ━━━━ ━━━━ can be developed with the following exercises. The diminuendo will be more difficult to sing than the crescendo, and every effort must be made to return to piano each time.

Choirs should learn to disassociate forte from higher pitches. The following exercises may assist with this problem.

The following techniques should be used to further increase the choir's awareness of dynamics:

1. Practice some easy compositions with a *swallowed hum*. This vocal production should be done with full support but at a barely audible level. When a true pianissimo is secure, sing with words. Try to retain the sensation of humming and keep the very soft dynamic.

2. Practice fortissimo singing with isolated chords from a composition. Make sure there is no forcing, tension, or harsh quality apparent. In building fortissimo, emphasize the bass. Work to produce a structure in the proportions shown in Figure 4.7a; that is, in seeking to create a fortissimo, build it up from the lower voices, rather than the more common way shown in Figure 4.7b.

FIGURE 4.7

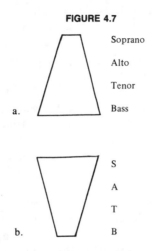

3. Ask different parts to sing different dynamic levels, such as basses *f,* all others *p;* bass and soprano *p,* tenor and alto, *f,* and so on.

4. Ask full sections to balance a solo voice in another section—for example, a single bass singer and a full section of sopranos, altos, and tenors. Potential imbalance in choirs caused by disproportionate numbers of personnel can be overcome to a considerable extent by learning to balance to the smaller section. This technique works much better than trying to force the small section to sing louder.

5. Many choral singers disregard the printed dynamic indications. Be sure they know the meaning of, and heed every mark on, the page of music. Give particular attention to *p, pp,* ⎯⎯⎯ , ⎯⎯⎯ , subito *p, sfz.*

6. Have fun practicing the *Doppler effect,* the sound of an approaching, passing, and departing automobile.

   f

   Work to produce a long zoom ----------------------------- ; keep it even.

TEXT

The principal factor that distinguishes choral music from instrumental music is the use of words to carry the tones of the composition. In this factor is found an additional component. Instrumental music can suggest moods, give delight by color contrasts, and provide a sense of aesthetic satisfaction as an evolving musical form is consummated; it cannot convey a specific idea. By means of the text, choral music can deliver a message or statement of praise, love, hate, fear, and so on. It can carry scenic descriptions and objectively narrate a series of events. Although it is essentially the tone and not the text that carries the emotion, it is nevertheless very important that as many of the words as possible be made clear to the listener.

Admittedly, it is not always possible for the text to be understood clearly. Two or three lines of counterpoint usually create a cloud of out-of-line syllables which make it impossible to understand the words. Long melismatic passages and sustained tones in high registers are also frequently unintelligible. Yet, even in these cases it is often possible to deliver the words intact, for the first statement of the fugue subject usually stands forth quite unencumbered, and if some high voices sustain lines that lose their textual clarity, lower voices may at the same time have an opportunity to deliver the text. In chorales and other homophonic styles there is no reason why *every* word should not be clearly understood.

As in the case of tone, the individual conductor's concern for clarity of text varies greatly. Some directors never mention the words; others scold their singers for not "enunciating" clearly, but give no specific aids or directives. Others build their entire concept of choral tone and artistry on the words. Probably the wisest approach is somewhere in the middle. Words are important and should be understood. Proper attention to the details of speech can have a beneficial effect on the pitch and tone of a choir. Great vocal-choral music is not, however, a mere highlighting of text. Singing is far more than heightened, sustained speech. The music is an independent structure, closely allied to but nevertheless separate from the words. Although either text or music is usually subservient, both must be capable of standing alone. Both work together, but if a choice must be made between musical and speech factors, the music must be served first. Matters of pulse, duration, and phrasing are more important to the overall musical conception than is an occasional misplaced syllable.

Therefore, granting that careful attention to the principles of good speech will enhance the choir's pitch perception, rhythmic acuity, and sense of phrasing, our goal in this discussion is to improve the communication inherent in the text of a choral composition. It will not do at all, in spite of perfection of musical delivery, to regale an audience with ridiculous phrases such as "Lessus wed in thee wadder" or "Gum, all ye, sin to the Law."

Only the problems of speaking and singing in English will be considered here. It is hoped that the depth of this examination will inspire conductors and singers to examine their proficiency in other languages. As the majority of the people studying this book think, read, and speak English as their first language, it seems appropriate to start there.

The question often arises as to whether a choral work should be performed in the original language; there is no conclusive answer to this question. It is always interesting to hear the union of words and music as conceived by the composer; however, an extended composition in which neither performers nor audience understands in any detail what is happening is likely to be dull, regardless of how well the text is pronounced. Latin translated into English usually does not go well with the music, and translations of other languages frequently require alterations in the rhythm and phrasing of the original music. I personally advocate that short works be performed in the original language, ensuring that the singers know the meaning of every word and that members of the audience have a translated text. I always perform Latin texts in Latin with these same rules. Extended works such as cantatas and passions are usually more successful when given in the language of the majority of the performers and listeners.

In preparing to improve the textual communication of the choir, conductors should ask themselves a few pertinent questions:

1. Is there a definite message in the text? That is, is there a comprehensible story, descriptive situation, or drama? It is useless to polish up diction if no literary sense can be made from the results.

2. Do I know the full meaning of every word? Are there any differences between the current meaning of the word and the meaning as it was understood in the time of the composer? When, in *Elijah*, we cry "Extirpate the foe," do we know the meaning of the verb? Or, in Britten's *Rejoice in the Lamb*, do we know who Ishmael was? If we are singing in a language other than English, do we know the meaning of each individual word, as well as the general thought of the poem? It is not possible to give the full impact inherent in the cries of *suscipe* in the "Gloria" of Haydn's *Mass in Time of War* unless we can tell our singers exactly what they are calling out.

3. Do I pronouce each word correctly, regardless of the language being used? Every choral conductor needs large dictionaries in several languages to consult regularly. In this day of mumblers, we all may be guilty of errors or omissions. *Twenty* is not *twenny* or *tweddy*, nor is *English, Inglish*. *Mary, merry*, and *marry* are not pronounced the same way.

The conductor must serve as a model of correct pronunciation, enunciation, and articulation and must be a master of dramatic expression. To accomplish these ends, he or she should read the text aloud as many times as is necessary to secure a complete understanding of the message, to realize the full dramatic impact of the lines, and to polish and perfect an oral delivery of the text. Hearing yourself by means of a recording may be a revelation!

In teaching the choir members to sing with clear diction, the conductor will frequently encounter a problem whose roots lie in the method by which we were taught to read. Many people learned to read by a procedure sometimes described as "look-say." They were shown, for example, a picture of a boy jumping over a lighted candle and they saw the words *Jack, candle,* and *jump*. They built up their vocabulary by remembering the *shape* of hundreds of words. They never sounded out parts of words, nor, possibly, did they learn the alphabet. The method worked well for some, who now read very rapidly and can get the message of entire paragraphs with a few glances through it. However, they may be likely to confuse syllables in unfamiliar words and have difficulty with spelling. Many others never learned to read fluently because they could not remember the hundreds of patterns.

Germane to our discussion here is the fact that many people are not cognizant of the various sounds *within* a word. A first step in securing good diction in a choir is to make the singers keenly aware of the breakdown of each word. Initial emphasis is, therefore, not upon the *words*, but upon the *syllables*, and all the sounds within each syllable.

For example, *toot* has two different sounds. The principal part of the word is the vowel $\overline{oo}$, which is preceded and followed by a *t*. If *toot* is sung, the vowel takes the pitch of the note indicated. There is no pitch to the *t* sound and it takes only a microsecond to sound it. *Moon* presents other problems. The vowel is $\overline{oo}$, as in *toot*, but the initial *m* and the concluding *n* have pitch and must be given more time in order that they may sound. If *toot* is sung to a half note, little thought is required as to the rhythmic dispositon of the three sounds, but *moon* to a half note will become something like this:

m - oo - n

It will not do to sing

m - oo - n

or

m - oo - n____

unless a special effect is desired.

Music notation would become impossibly and needlessly complicated if an attempt were made to set every sound of every vowel to its own note, so it is the conductor's responsibility to determine exactly when each sound is to be made and to instruct the choir, if necessary. Time should not be wasted in needless explanations; many complicated rhythmic combinations of sounds fall into place naturally through habits of speech.

Vowels

As the major part (possibly 95 percent) of every syllable is taken up by the vowel, it is apparent that a good starting place for the development of precise choral diction is in the isolation and clarification of each vowel sound. The singers must know exactly what vowel they are trying to sing; everyone must be together on this point. The members of the choir must become aware of *pure* vowel sounds. Lack of this awareness is the basis of much faulty singing and poor diction. As the conductor seeks to unify the singers on this point, two problems immediately arise: (1) regional differences in pronunciation (*amen, ahmen,* and *awmen,* for example) and (2) the inability of many people to differentiate between similar vowel sounds. I recall one singer who could not hear or produce an appreciable difference between the principal sounds of *sun (ŭ), far (ä),* and *law (ô).* Indeed, *ä* and *ô* are frequently confused, as are *ōō (boot)* and *yōō (pew).*

The vowel chart on page 96 will be valuable in teaching the choir to hear and produce cleanly a series of vowel sounds which will suffice for most problems of choral singing in English. Not all the English vowels are included, as our task would be unnecessarily complicated if we tried to teach the twenty or more sounds indicated in most dictionaries. Each vowel is identified by a key word (*best, far, go,* and so on) and by the diacritical marking used in pronunciation guides (*ĕ, ä, ō,* and so on). The vowels are arranged to proceed from thin sounds on the left to round sounds on the right. The primary vowel sounds are placed in squares; the subordinate sounds, in circles. Descending from the central vowel sound *ah (far, ä),* are two subordinate sounds vital to English diction which require special consideration and treatment: *uh (sofa, ə)* and *er (term, û).*

To introduce the chart to the choir, it would be well to begin with the primary vowel sounds in a five-tone scale pattern:

mee	may	mah	moh	moo
nee	nay	nah	noh	noo
bee	bay	bah	boh	boo

Next move to chords, singing the five sounds on each chord.

nee, nay, nah, noh, noo   *etc.,*   *etc.*

The conductor should ensure that the singers move smoothly from one vowel to the next and that the pitch does not drop as the vowels change from light to dark. Every effort should be made for unification in the sound. It is often revealing to have each person in a section sing alone. Common problems are singing *my (mī)* for *may (mā), maw (mô)* for *mah (mä),* and *mew (myōō)* for *moo (mōō).*

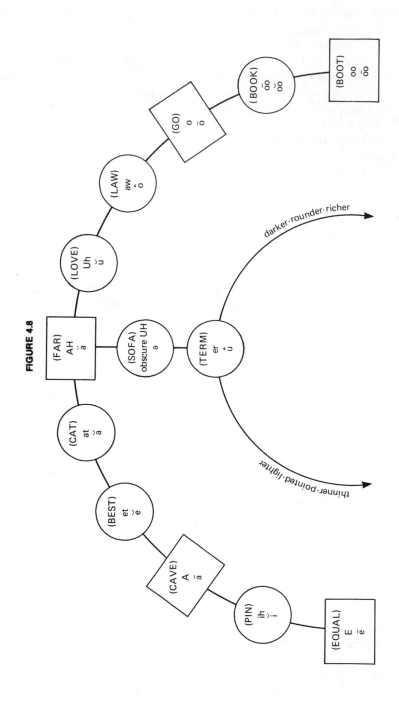

FIGURE 4.8

The primary vowel sounds should be thoroughly drilled until perfected in five-tone scales, chords, and exercises. Work should be done in major and minor modes at various dynamic levels in the middle, most comfortable part of the voice.

When the choir sings these five vowel exercises, the conductor should ascertain that as the singers strive to create pure sounds, there is a smooth flow of *color* from one vowel to the next. At no time should the five vowels sound as if they were sung by five different people. Vowel phonation requires little lip movement; vowel changes are made mostly in the throat. The vowels should meld into each other and, at the same time, retain their own purity.

Once these five primary vowel sounds have become well set in the choristers' technique, it is not difficult to move to the subordinate vowels, those sounds in the circles on the chart. The primary sounds serve as anchor points from which movement may be securely made. The chorus might sing *cave* ($\overline{a}$) and then move the sound gently to *best* ($\breve{e}$). This might be followed by singing *cave best* several times and terminating with an alternation of the two vowel sounds without an initial consonant: $\overline{a} - \breve{e} - \overline{a} - \breve{e} - \overline{a} - \breve{e}$ In a similar manner, *far* ($\ddot{a}$) might be followed by and then alternated with *cat* ($\breve{a}$). If this is successful, try singing *cave best cat far* ($\overline{a} - \breve{e} - \breve{a} - \ddot{a}$), making four clean, distinctly different vowel sounds. Little by little the entire arch should be filled in until the singers can negotiate the passage from *equal* ($\overline{e}$) to *boot* ($\overline{oo}$) and back again with eleven distinct sounds.

Two subordinate vowel sounds are the obscure English vowel ə as in the unstressed sound in *sofa* and *about,* and the *er* sound in *term* or *serve,* usually indicated as $\hat{u}$ in pronunciation guides. They are placed below the $\ddot{a}$ on the chart, and it would be best to approach them from a word such as *far.*

The *stressed* sound *uh* ($\breve{u}$) as in *love* and *son* requires strong support of the singing muscles. It should never be allowed to become vague in its focus and assume an exclamation of stupidity: *duuh!* In the following phrase the $\breve{u}$ in *son* and *come* should be energized.

In an *unstressed* position, however, *uh* is the obscure English vowel ə as in *sofa* or *about.* Although ə is slightly less intense than $\breve{u}$, it must, nevertheless, have vitality. The contrast between ə and $\breve{u}$ can be experienced by the singing of the following firmly:

In most choral situations it is very difficult to hear a significant difference between the two sounds $\breve{u}$ and ∂.

In certain geographic areas of North America the vowel sound *er (ûr)* as in *term, serve,* and *learn* becomes very unpleasant because of excessive forward placement and nasality. This unpleasant sound is often mistakenly used for ∂ or other vowels in words such as *monitor (moń ∂ tər)* and *literature (lit 'ər-ə-choor),* which gratingly become *moń-ûr-tûr* and *lit'-ûr-ûr-chûr.* This tendency is especially noticeable in the Midwestern states. The *ûr* sound should be carefully drilled to take on some of the character of $\breve{u}$ *and* ∂ by the choir's progressing from those two vowel sounds into *ûr,* avoiding nasality or "twang."

As you are working through the primary vowel sounds in the square boxes ($\bar{e} - \bar{a} - \ddot{a} - \bar{o} - \overline{oo}$), it will become apparent that $\bar{a}$ *(cave)* and $\bar{o}$ *(go)* are unlike the other three in that there are two sounds to the vowel—a sustained sound and a vanishing sound. These two-sound vowels are called *diphthongs.* In addition to the two on the vowel chart, there are four more which we must examine.

KEY WORD	SUNG AS	MARKING
cow	k — <u>AH</u> OO	ou (ä + $\overline{oo}$)
sigh	s — <u>AH</u> EE	$\bar{\text{i}}$(ä + $\bar{e}$)
voice	v — <u>AW</u> EE-s	oi (ô + $\bar{e}$)
view	v — EE <u>OO</u>	y$\overline{oo}$ ($\bar{e}$ + $\overline{oo}$)
cave	k — <u>A</u> EE-v	$\bar{a}$ ($\bar{a}$ + $\bar{e}$)
go	g — <u>O</u> OO	$\bar{o}$ ($\bar{o}$ + $\overline{oo}$)

In the chart above, the sustained part of the diphthong is underlined. It must be firmly sounded and not allowed to "creep" into the vanishing vowel, which should be sounded cleanly, distinctly, and quickly after the sustaining vowel. (An exception is in the case of *y$\overline{oo}$,* where the vanishing vowel *precedes* the sustaining vowel.)

Diphthongs may be drilled as follows:

The figure ♩. ♪ gives the location and rhythmic placement of the vanishing part of *ou.*

The following phrases may be helpful in clarifying the remaining diphthongs.

The diphthong ee $\overline{oo}$ *(view, y$\overline{oo}$)* presents special problems. The vanishing part is very likely to be neglected in both speech and singing. This omission gives rise to provincialisms such as *t$\overline{oo}$z-d$\bar{e}$* for *ty$\overline{oo}$z-d$\bar{a}$*, and *d$\overline{oo}$k* for *dy$\overline{oo}$k*. Drill by speaking sentences such as, "The rehearsal has been moved to Tuesday *(t$\overline{oo}$ ty$\overline{oo}$z-d$\bar{a}$)*" and "Don't shoot *(sh$\overline{oo}$t)* the duke *(dy$\overline{oo}$k)*." Be aware that the vowel *u* following *d, l, n, s, t* and sometimes *m* often requires the diphthong *y$\overline{oo}$* rather than the vowel *$\overline{oo}$*. Consult your dictionary.

It should be apparent from this discussion of vowels that we are striving for a standard of English pronunciation that might be described as cosmopolitan, neither provincial nor affected, "a norm on the stage and in other public usage" (Madeline Marshall).[6] Your exclamation, "Oi hoit me oi!" or "Ah huht mah ah!" may immediately identify you as a native of eastern Canada or southwestern United States, respectively. Your own accent is part

---

[6]Madeline Marshall, *The Singer's Manual of English Diction* (New York: G. Schirmer, Inc., 1953), p. 3.

of your heritage and is your own business. However, your choir should sing "I hurt my eye!" without a trace of regionalism. It's all in the vowel.

Consonants

As about 95 percent of the sounds made by a choir are vowels, they have a tremendous effect upon the tone. Because of this effect, many conductors concentrate almost exclusively upon the vowel sounds in order to bring them to the highest possible level of unification, purity, and polish. Thus the consonant sounds may be neglected, although without well-articulated and correctly placed consonants, intelligibility of the text is not possible.

Consonants may be grouped into three main categories: those that have no definite pitch, such as *f* and *t;* those that have a sustainable pitch, such as *m* and *v;* and those that have a barely noticeable, fragmentary pitch, such as *b* and *d.*

Consonants belonging to each of these categories are listed below.

Consonants having no pitch

C   —center, call
CH—chop, chess
F   —fit, fun
H   —hold, harm
K   —kick, kitten
P   —put, pop
Q   —queen, quest
S   —snow, sea
SH —ship, show
T   —toot, top
TH (unvoiced) — thin, thought
WH—who, wheat

Consonants with sustainable pitch

L   —lot, long
M   —moon, Mary
N   —not, now
NG—sing, among
R   —rise, run
S (as Z) — is, frisbee
TH (voiced) — then, that
V   —vent, vault
W   —wise, weep
X (as Z) — xanadu, xerox
Z   —zoo, zeal
ZH —azure, pleasure

Consonants with fragmentary pitch

B — boy, bring   G — God, get
D — dog, dance   J — jump, jail

In helping the choir to become more aware of consonants, it might be best to start with those of sustainable pitch. Construct a four-part chord with a comfortable note for each voice and have the choir slowly sing the key words from the list. Make each consonant sound very long to ensure that the singers experience the sensation of a sustained sound.

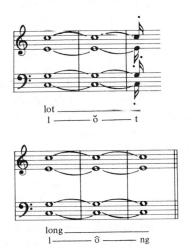

As the choir works through the list of words in this manner, it will become apparent that some of the sustained consonants have a relatively unpleasant and unmusical sound, such as *v (vent)*. Others are only moderately raspy—*z (zoo)* or *r (run)*—and some are among the most beautiful of all singing sounds, bursting with resonance and vitality—*m (moon), n (not),* and *ng (sing).*

Having experimented with all the sustainable consonant sounds and realizing that they must be clearly heard and that care must be taken in establishing their pitch, the conductor and the singers, drawing upon their own good taste, will decide to what degree each must be emphasized in the music. This emphasis is accomplished both by the amount of time given to the consonant (duration) and by the dynamic level (loudness). Beyond making this suggestion, it seems pointless to draw up specific rules, although some directives regarding pitch and rhythm will be given later.

Let us turn next to the pitchless consonants. If the choir speaks or sings these words slowly, the singers will hear that some of the letters have an explosive quality which can be sounded at a precise moment—*c (call)* or *t (toot).* This precision is accomplished with a flick of the tongue or a pop of the lips. Other nonpitch consonants require more time to sound and are characterized by an aspirated sound of rushing wind—*f (fit)* or *c (center)*. The conductor will need to spend considerable time in encouraging the singers to make the unvoiced wind sounds audible, for vocalists often fear that they will lose too much breath in so doing. With the variation in time required to sound the pitchless consonants, it is obvious that there are potential problems here in regard to the security of the rhythm. This point will be discussed later. At the present it will suffice to have the singers work through the list of pitchless consonants, ensuring that a clean sound is made for each one.

In the case of *b, d, g,* and *j,* it must be understood that they possess characteristics of both pitch and nonpitch consonants. Each of these letters is closely related to a pitchless consonant—*b* to *p, d* to *t, g* to *k,* and *j* to *ch.* For the most part, *b, d, g,* and *j* function as explosive, pitchless consonants, similar to their relatives *p, t, k,* and *ch.* The lips and tongue are in the same position for each pair of letters. However, the distinction lies in the fact that when *b, d, g,* or *j* are sounded correctly at the beginning of a word, there is a brief, pitched sound, low in the throat. Some people have difficulty hearing this subvocal sound, which seems to be slightly easier to hear with *b.* It is essential that this low sound be clearly identified and sounded, however briefly, at the pitch of the vowel that follows. Omission of this fragmentary, subvocal sound causes *boy* to be heard as *poy, dog* becomes *tog,* and so on. When *b, d, g,* or *j* are placed at the *end* of a word, a touch of the obscure vowel *uh* (ə) must be added to produce intelligibility. Otherwise, *god (god-uh)* becomes *got, rib (rib-uh)* becomes *rip,* and *David (David-uh)* becomes *Davit.*

Rehearsal time devoted to clarifying the problems of *b, d, g,* and *j* is well spent. Improper execution of these letters is often responsible for wavering pitch, rhythmic insecurity, and poor diction. The conductor should be certain they are well understood by all the singers.

General Rules for Diction

As we have now examined the principal components of speech—vowels and consonants—it is possible to formulate some general rules for the application of words or syllables to musical lines.

1. Sing every sound in each syllable.
2. Sing every vowel with absolute clearness. Do not allow the vowel to "creep" or change during the time it is held. The vowel must remain pure.
3. Do not neglect the vanishing part of the diphthongs.
4. Activate the consonants and strive for textual communication, but do not permit the pronunciation to become "affected."
5. Ensure that each sound is rhythmically and securely placed on a pulse or subdivision thereof. Each sound must be in its own "time slot."
6. As the pulse is the main factor in maintaining the forward motion of the music, and as the vocal sound is carried principally by the vowels, it is apparent that each pulse must be marked precisely by the sounding of a vowel. The only exception to this rule would be in the case of precise, exploded consonants—*k,*

t, and so on. As they require but a microsecond to sound, they are useful in clarifying the exact moment of the pulse. *B, d, g,* and *j* may also come on the beat.

7. All other consonant sounds, those of sustained pitch, as well as the aspirated, pitchless ones, are sounded off the beat. Indeed, they sound best that way.

8. Listen critically to the effect of the ensemble singing the aspirated consonants. It may be necessary to intensify some and subdue others. *S,* for example, can be quite objectionable when sung by a large choir.

9. Give *m, n,* and *ng* a longer time value than the other tuned consonants. It is sometimes helpful to think of *mm, nn,* and *nng.*

10. Higher pitches require some modification of the vowels as well as less emphasis on the tuned consonants. Good vocal production takes precedence over precise diction at high pitches.

Tuning the pitch consonants frequently causes difficulties. The following rules may assist with this activity:

1. Read the text slowly. Underline the sustainable pitch consonants and determine their pitch.

2. Pitch consonants frequently, but not always, are sounded on the pitch of the vowels that follow them.

is sung:

The tempo will affect the duration of *l,* but it must be intoned on B♭ *prior* to the beat, at which point we should hear the vowel. *R* comes as indicated, on the second half of the third beat; at a very slow tempo, it might become ♪ rather than ♪. *D,* followed by ə, comes on the fourth beat precisely.

3. When a tuned consonant is preceded by a vowel of a different pitch, the consonant is usually tuned to that pitch.

is sung:

The subvocal sound preceding B must come before the beat on the pitch of $\bar{e}$. The explosive *B* comes exactly on the beat. The *m* of *mine* is sung on the pitch of F, not B^b, for at that point we must hear the vowel $\ddot{a}$. The vanishing part of the diphthong is sounded quickly on the same pitch as the sustained portion, as is the *n*. The final *e* of *mine* is silent. Once again, the tempo will affect the rhythmic proportions. Those given above are for moderato.

To produce continuity of thought, the text must flow. The following rules for continuity may clarify this point:

1. Except when staccato and marcato articulations are required, move positively from syllable to syllable and word to word. Beware holes in the line; strive for connectedness. Teach your choir the meaning of legato; beware of *marching!*
2. Punctuation marks provide a guide to the musical phrasing.
3. A period in the text usually calls for a stop in the flow of tone. Breath may or may not be taken.
4. A comma *may* require a stop in the tone, but beware of too many breaks in the line.
5. Repeated words or phrases are often made clearer by stopping the tone for an instant. Tempo and setting are determining factors.

6. A vocative (one addressed) should usually be followed by a break in the tone.

7. In all other cases, work for a strong continuity of tone from syllable to syllable and from word to word. However, beware of connections that would cause misunderstandings in the text.

   Let us in　　should not become *Lettusin*

   For unto us　should not become *Foruntowus*

8. Having the choir whisper the text in rhythm will reveal weak points in the diction. Whispering is excellent for obtaining clear consonants and intensity, as is intoning the text on a single pitch.

EFFICIENT REHEARSALS

Needless to say, the conductor must develop skill in applying the five choral techniques to the ensemble. Attention should be given, *as needed,* to the five techniques in fairly equal proportion. Beware laboring points; change the emphasis regularly throughout the rehearsal.

The following 50 guidelines may be of assistance to the conductor in developing efficient rehearsals.

1. Before the first rehearsal you must thoroughly digest the music that is to be presented. Allow a period of time to permit the composition to mature in your thought. Review the procedures listed on pages 18–19.

2. Go over the music with the rehearsal pianist before the singers assemble. The rehearsal is not the place to correct the pianist's wrong notes or lack of understanding of the style.

3. Arrive early for each rehearsal and ascertain that all logistics are in order.

4. All singers must be aware that they have a definite contribution to make to the choral body and that their invariable presence is vital to every rehearsal. The singer who occasionally drops in to sing, or last-minute "ringers" who are added to bolster a potentially disastrous concert, contribute little and may well detract from the overall growth of the choir.

5. All singers should have their own music. If several compositions are being rehearsed, they should be in a folder marked with the chorister's name. Each singer needs a pencil with which to notate the conductor's directions.

6. Indicate on a chalk board or bulletin board the compositions that are to be studied at each rehearsal. Choristers should get the compositions in order before the rehearsal begins. Constantly guard against wasting time.

7. Someone besides the conductor should take the attendance, distribute music, set up chairs, and so on. Assigning these important duties to members of the choir can provide a sense of active participation to those involved. You should be free to concentrate on the rehearsal of the music.

8. Begin and conclude the rehearsal exactly at the appointed hours. In so doing, you show your respect for the commitment of time your singers have given you. Do not tolerate chronic tardiness or early leaving.

9. Usually, vocalize the choir with various exercises before starting to rehearse the music. Five to ten minutes of this work can do much to improve the rehearsal. However, occasionally use an easy composition as the warm-up.

10. Routines can be deadly. Work for variety in the warm-ups and rehearsal procedures. Each rehearsal should include some review or further study of previously rehearsed material, a run-through of a section or a complete composition that is well learned, and an introduction to some new music. Vary the order in which you take up these three items. It is especially important for a choir regularly to read new works. Try immediately to apply the technical and artistic principles that are being developed in the regular rehearsals. Work toward a climax to conclude each rehearsal, sometimes powerfully dramatic, sometimes quietly reflective.

11. Try to begin each rehearsal with something that will go well. Give the choir a sense of satisfaction right at the onset. Then move to new or difficult material.

12. Practice having the choir respond vigorously and audibly to your preparatory beat until *everyone* understands the necessity for breathing together in the tempo and character of what is to follow. Get the engine running freely before the clutch is engaged.

13. It is *vital* for *every* performer and the conductor to be in eye contact during the preparatory beat. Insist on this point.

14. Develop in your singers the ability to understand the technical language of music. Teach them music terminology.

15. Guard against over-conducting or attempting to inspire your singers to great artistic heights during the initial study of a composition. Learn the notes first. Conduct the singers cleanly from beat to beat. Conductors often conduct too much; concentrate on critical listening.

16. You must have eye-to-eye contact with your singers constantly. If you expect them to communicate with you, you must communicate with them. Do not bury your head in the score, and do not permit your singers to do so either.

17. Train your choir to locate quickly the spot you wish to rehearse; say, for example, "Page 20, third system, second measure, fourth beat." The pianist should *immediately* sound the pitches—bass, tenor, alto, soprano—without further instruction from you. Keep this procedure constant; keep the rehearsal moving.

18. Initially, insist that the singers learn to observe every mark on the printed page. Teach them to be cognizant of tempo indications, articulation marks, fermatas, slurs, repeat signs, and so on. Many choristers look only at the words. Later, if changes are made, they should be notated on the page. Use pencils freely!

19. When learning parts, especially in music of the Baroque and Renaissance periods where a sectional sound is desirable, separate the four sections of the choir into the four corners of the room. Have each section stand in a circle and sing across to the person opposite.

20. Train the choir to be able to start at any point on the page. Do not always start at easy spots.

21. After the initial reading of a new work, immediately begin to correct mistakes. Remember the five techniques. Do not allow errors to be rehearsed into the music. Practice the most difficult sections. Beware singing through, time and time again, the parts that are well learned and secure.

22. Sing for your group. Demonstrate your wishes. Be concise and concrete in your directives.

23. As far as possible, scrutinize the four sections of the choir equally. Do not be guilty of ignoring the altos, picking on the tenors, and so on. All the sections expect your leadership.

24. Urge the choir members to begin to memorize at once. Allow time for the composition to mature in the singers' minds.

25. You must never become passive; you must constantly *take action*. Deliver a steady flow of reminders and directives to your forces. You must *transmit* constantly; do not coast.

26. Do not be a bluffer. Admit your mistakes. However, too many blunders may be an indication of insufficient preparation.

27. Encourage your singers to free themselves from the printed notes as soon as possible. Many singers continue to reread the notes even after they know them. After learning the notes, sing the music. There is a difference.

28. Frequently have the choir stand up, stretch, and move about. Be alert to physical lethargy in your choir.

29. Ask the choir to sing something from memory at each rehearsal. Try to conduct as long as possible without looking at your score. Memory work is vital for both conductors and singers. It is not necessary, however, to sing concerts from memory; the time can be better spent learning more music. Nevertheless, the printed music must, as soon as possible, be relegated to a position where it is used for reference only.

30. During every rehearsal you must have regular eye-to-eye contact with every singer and player.

31. When rehearsing, do not try to hear everything at the same time unless you have an extremely keen ear and extensive conducting experience. It is better to listen for specifics. Rotate your concentration among the five techniques—pitch, rhythm, tone, dynamics, and text.

32. A short recess in the middle of a rehearsal may be beneficial. However, guard against losing the momentum. It may be better to have the choir stand, move about, or sing something in a different style. Announcements or other business might be transacted at this time.

33. For fun and reading experience, occasionally have sections sing other parts—sopranos sing bass part (in soprano range, of course), basses sing alto (octave lower), and so on. In so doing, reading improves and singers become much more cognizant of other sections of the choir.

34. Do not harangue your choir. Give praise when praise is due.

35. Try to have at least one good laugh at each rehearsal. Keep the singers in good humor.

36. Read new music regularly. Constantly refresh the weary spirit of your singers by bringing them stimulating literature.

37. If you utilize instrumentalists with your choir, get them up to the level of the singers. Build up the orchestra as you have the choir. Rehearse the players separately if possible.

38. The orchestra players must breathe, in their minds, at the upbeat. The orchestra and the choir will then attack together.

39. The orchestra must respond to the conductor's downbeat; if it does not, the attacks will become later and later. Keep discipline in your orchestra as you have in your choir.

40. Maintain a good dynamic balance between the players and singers at all times. Mark down the dynamic levels in the brass parts. If the strings are too loud, instruct the players to bow closer to the fingerboard rather than near the bridge.

41. Regularly record your rehearsals. Study the tapes. Do you rehearse efficiently? If possible, videotape your rehearsals. Show the results to your choir.

42. At the core of every great ensemble is the ability to play and sing in a chamber style, with extreme sensitivity to one another. Therefore, regularly break the choir down into small ensembles or quartets. Have these small groups demonstrate for each other.

43. Occasionally, spread the entire choir in a scrambled formation around the perimeter of a large room. Singing in this arrangement builds confidence and sonority.

44. Do not over-rehearse. When a composition has been brought up to the highest level of excellence possible, perform it and/or give it a rest. Excessive rehearsing may cause a composition to deteriorate.

45. Do not talk too much. Remember: you are there to make music.

46. At times, walk around through the various sections of the choir while they are singing. You may be pleasantly surprised or dismayed at what you hear.

47. Occasionally, let someone else conduct. Sit back and listen objectively to your own choir. Have they been well instructed? Do they lean on you personally?

48. At dress rehearsals, try to simulate the actual performance conditions. Leave nothing to chance.

49. Record your concerts for future study. However, do not play the tapes immediately after the performance; it is often a letdown to do so. Do not hold a long, boring postmortem at the rehearsal following a concert. A few words of appreciation to your forces may be very much in order, but extended analysis of past disasters or triumphs accomplishes little. Turn immediately to new music.

50. Either love your choir or leave it.

CHAPTER FIVE
CHORAL ARTISTRY

The techniques and exercises set forth in the previous chapters, if applied conscientiously and regularly to a choral organization in which improvement and growth are at all possible, should produce performances that are at least respectable. By this I mean that the pitches and rhythms of the printed score will be accurately reproduced, that there will be a well-supported, flexible, active tone, that the composer's wishes regarding tempo, dynamics, and other marks of expression will be observed, and that the text of the compositions will come through clearly to the audience. In short, through the efforts of the chorus members who have not only been *drilled* by their conductor but also *taught,* a clean, literal translation of the printed score into sound will be accomplished. At this point, the choir will have arrived at what is sometimes referred to as the "learned-note" stage.

Such a level of choral experience, although rather meager if compared to artistic performances given by professional choirs, is by no means to be despised; many choral ensembles never reach the "learned-note, clean-sound" level. Countless school and church choirs continue year after year with singers who show no sign of growth, either vocally or in musical understanding. Their rehearsals are given over largely to banging out (literally) the parts on the piano. Most performances are characterized by the same bland, boring tone, intonation that ranges from poor to horrible, and words that are poured forth in a monotone of garbled vowels and nonexistent consonants. These singing groups, scarcely deserving to be called choirs, are the result of the conductors' ineptitude—an ignorance of, or disinterest in, vocal-choral techniques.

Almost any group of singers can achieve technical proficiency if well taught, and if this level is gained, the way is prepared for greater events. If creative, artistic leadership is then not available to advance the choir beyond this stage, the organization can at least be assured that, with its secure technique, it will never give embarrassing performances. Although excellence in choral techniques by no means ensures the development of choral artistry, it is scarcely possible for an artistic choral experience to arise from a shaky technical foundation. True, in the history of musical performance there have been some very great artists who were champion hitters of wrong notes; a superior grasp of artistic principles *can* enhance the technique. However, in developing a choir, conductors should not slight the technical preparation of the singers in favor of the less tangible factors of artistry, expressivity, or whatever you choose to call it. There are great pitfalls for a choir that attempts to perform expressively without thoroughly knowing the notes; in most choral situations the artistic choral experience begins *after* the learned-note, technical stage has been reached.

What is an "artistic choral experience"? Certainly, we are all familiar with the phenomenon of the technically correct musical performance which fails to move us. Such performances may be labeled cold, uninspiring, or just plain dull. The performers may be accused of lacking musical sensitivity or of simply failing to "get into the music."

Music teachers frequently try to advance their pupils beyond the learned-note level of music making by asking the student to *imitate,* the procedure being, "No, no, my dear, play it this way!" Conductors strive (sometimes successfully) to inspire or propel their forces to artistic heights by humor, colorful speeches, bodily gyrations, and tantrums. A teacher whose pupils play without expression is often dismissed as a "technique freak"; a conductor whose forces perform correctly but in an uninspiring manner may be said to lack "fire from heaven" or, more frequently, to be "unmusical."

These well-known, vague terms with which performers and listeners attempt to describe their dissatisfaction with a musical experience that is merely technically correct are typical of the entire approach to the level of music making that can occur after the notes are learned. There is often confusion in listeners' minds between what they *hear* and what they *feel.* Performances riddled with wrong notes, but feelingfully presented, are acceptable to some people but are intolerable to others. There is a curious reluctance on the part of musicians to talk about artistry or expressiveness. Questions concerning this level of musical performance are often answered with equally vague or inconclusive remarks such as, "I just feel it," or "I've never thought much about it," or "I just play loud or soft, fast or slow, whatever I'm told." There is a widespread feeling that artistry, like conducting, can be neither taught nor learned—you either have it or you do not. Not uncommon also is the rather irritatingly priggish outlook that if one has to inquire about artistry it will not be recognized when it is found.

What is this "musicality," this "fire from heaven," this mysterious something which sets apart the artist from the technician? Is there tangible information on this subject which can be analyzed, discussed, and taught to choir members? Can a choir progress beyond the stage of merely correctly rendering the printed page? Certainly. We have all heard it happen. Some conductors invariably produce fine choral concerts, regardless of the forces they are conducting. Interestingly enough, many conductors are unable to explain what they do when they bring a group up to a high level of choral artistry.

I believe that any choir that has mastered the fundamental vocal and choral techniques can, with the right leadership, advance into the artistic stages of choral performance. If the conductor and the singers are willing to work on the problems of artistry as diligently as they tackled the problems of pitch, rhythm, and speech, they will be able to reach high levels of inspiration and achieve deeply expressive, musical experiences. The task of developing artistry in the choir is somewhat more difficult than the problems of technique, but achieving artistic performances produces a lasting satisfaction which far transcends the sense of accomplishment coming from simply getting the notes in shape.

"What does one do to get beyond the notes?" The answer is not simple. Several factors are involved, but, to put it in the most simple terms, *artistry* is essentially the bringing forth of sensitive elements which are *not* engraved on the printed page. Despite the importance of clean, correct sounds from the choir, the *essence* of choral music (or of any music, for that matter) is not found in correct pitches, rhythms, consonants, and so on. Nor can the intrinsic qualities of choral music be captured on paper. The words and tones convey the composer's *thoughts*. Even with the refinement of musical notation and the ever-growing mass of detailed printed instruction, the musical score cannot be more than a blueprint which *guides* the performer in the re-creation of the *music*. Musical performance is dependent upon both the technique *and* the artistry of the performers. Just as the conductor taught the choir members the techniques of vocal production and choral ensemble, so must the conductor give guidance in the development of their sensitivity to artistry. At this level of music making, the conductor is dealing almost exclusively with *subtleties*. A distinguishing trait of artistry is refinement, sensitivity to barely perceptible changes in tone, rhythm, and dynamics. The conductor must be a sensitive person and be able to convey these refinements to the singers.

There are basically three areas of study that contribute to the development of artistry in the performance of choral music. Like the five choral techniques, these three areas are all interrelated and act upon each other. They are also closely allied to and dependent upon the five techniques. Indeed, some conductors may think of portions of these areas of choral artistry as refinements or extensions of technique. Nevertheless, we will consider each one separately. All three are equally important, and the knowledgeable choral conductor will draw as necessary upon these three areas in advancing the choir as an artistic entity. These three areas of choral artistry are: (1) concern for historical accuracy regarding the period in which the music was composed and first performed; this area is often referred to as a study and appropriate execution of the *style* of the music; (2) a development of awareness toward subtle factors of rhythm and dynamics as they affect the *phrasing* of the music; and (3) learning to perceive and to project in its entirety the meaning, argument, and drama of a composition through heightened understanding of speech and tone as exemplified by performers of the theater.

HISTORICAL ACCURACY—STYLE

Excellent research has been accomplished in the field of musicology, making it possible to obtain with ease highly accurate information on performance practices in any period of music history. We are able to make logical assumptions concerning the tone which singers used in the sixteenth century; we know roughly how many players and singers J. S. Bach utilized when he first presented the *Passion According to St. Matthew;* and we know that the famous "Gloria" from the *Twelfth Mass* of Mozart is spurious, possibly having been composed by a pupil.

It is also encouraging to note that the more enlightened performers no longer consider these results of musical research as interesting but essentially useless information. We have learned that a detailed understanding of the conditions under which composers worked and directed, if we are willing to try to emulate those conditions, can result in greatly enhanced performances. For example, renditions of Handel's *Messiah* have in the past been characterized by choruses numbering hundreds of singers accompanied by a full orchestra with complete woodwind and brass sections. With the music thundering along, this is an impressive spectacle. In spite of my own fond recollection of some of these performances, I did not really grasp the spirit of *Messiah* nor experience the sheer joy of the melismatic solo and choral passages until I began to hear this oratorio performed with forces more like those Handel probably had in mind when composing the work.

It is not only in matters of performance conditions that we have become more enlightened. We can now obtain good publications of music which provide us with dependable, accurate printings devoid of anachronistic editings and superfluous additions. As a young music student, I sang a Palestrina mass in a large chorus accompanied by piano. The edition we used was filled with highly contrasting marks for dynamics and tempo which we meticulously observed. When the measure signature called for $\frac{4}{2}$ we delivered a march-like rhythm in slow half notes! In that ghastly performance. we gained no concept of the crystalline beauty of Palestrina's music. I doubt if our audience was greatly moved either; the music simply could not be heard through our massive ignorance of Renaissance style.

Of course, we can never duplicate exactly the original performance conditions; there must always be some compromise. Acoustics of concert halls are quite different from those of the cathedrals where the Renasissance masterworks were first heard; some tone colors such as those produced by the castrati no longer exist; and the entire sociological structure of our time—when we might dash home from the office, eat a heavy dinner, change into our concert-going attire (be it jeans and turtleneck or tuxedo), and take the subway or bus to hear a performance of a Gregorian mass by professional singers—bears little resemblance to the age when illiterate peasants, who might live their entire lives in the very shadow of the cathedral, obediently went to Mass, stood or knelt throughout the service, gazed on the spectacle, smelled the incense, and heard the music sung by men whose entire lives had been consecrated to serving the Church.

Nevertheless, conductors today have no excuse for using shoddy, inaccurate editions of music, for proclaiming ignorance of the performance conditions under which compositions were initially presented, for depending upon instinct rather than research for the proper execution of ornamentation, and for dismissing the entire subject of style as too personal or scholarly to be of interest to a real musician. A choral conductor who performs the motets of Bach and Brahms or a Haydn mass and Verdi's *Requiem* with identical forces and with the same sound is displaying a lack of artistry. Conductors who are unwilling to study and avail themselves of the labors of fine scholars should limit their conducting to innocuous compositions by unknown composers. Failure to display scholarship as a conductor limits the musical growth of the audience, the performers, and the director personally.

It is not possible within the confines of this book to present a full discussion of the musical styles of the past 500 years. Many excellent books on the subject are listed in the Bibliography (pp. 142–46), and the artistic conductor would do well to study all of them. However, for the benefit of conductors who are just beginning to encounter this aspect of artistic choral singing, the following pages contain a few general suggestions which may serve as a guide to performance of choral music from the Renaissance and the Baroque periods. These principles are distilled from the research and writing of several notable musicologists and conductors, and they in no way represent the total information available on each period. They have been exhaustively tested in many choirs.

The Renaissance Period: 1425–1600

Pitch. In the Renaissance, the pitch at which compositions were performed was not nearly as standardized as it is today. From one geographic location to another, our present A (440 vibrations per second) might be sounded as much as a third higher or lower. Scholarly editions of Renaissance music now usually indicate the level at which the notation was originally made; I do not believe that it is necessary to follow slavishly the interval of transposition advocated by modern editors. There are simply too many variables. Performances of specific compositions in the Renaissance certainly were given at various pitch levels, and modern, artistic conductors would do well to experiment to find the point at which the music sounds best. Two primary considerations should be the characteristics of the performers' voices and the acoustics of the auditorium in which the music is presented. Young voices, especially if the bass is light, may be able to present the lines more clearly if the pitch is somewhat higher than indicated on the modern score; on the other hand, an auditorium with little resonance may require the pitch to be lower in order to achieve an appropriate tone. The conductor should make a choice for the choir after careful thought, basing this decision on a concept of the score as discussed in Chapter 2.

It has already been mentioned that it is good training for a choir to practice compositions in different keys. If this advice has been followed, the singers are well equipped to participate in this interesting aspect of Renaissance performance.

Rhythm. Renaissance music is rhythmically much freer than music of the Baroque and later. Stress on important words or syllables controls the accents, which may or may not fall into a regular pattern. Measure lines did not exist in the Renaissance; any attempt to conduct music from this period with a traditional conducting pattern will result in a metrical accent, which will usually destroy the lines as conceived. A phrase may begin at any point in relation to another phrase. If the phrase begins with an accented word or syllable (for example, *gloria),* the accent may fall at any point within a "measure" as set up by a modern editor. Emphasis is also achieved by extended duration of a note as well as by higher pitches. Care must be taken that points of stress do not destroy the strong forward flow of the music.

Tempo is determined largely by the text and must be flexible but not with extremes of contrast. Especially to be avoided is the tendency to sing slowly simply because the notation is largely in white notes. Renaissance composers produced the effect of slowing down by lengthening note values. Therefore, it is inappropriate to also make ritards except at the very end of movements; this double-action slowdown would seriously distort the music.

Conductors must also be alert to changes of meter whereby a regular pulse continues but with different subdivisions. The most common change of this type is $\frac{4}{4}$ to $\frac{3}{4}$ and the quarter note is *not* constant; in this situation, the usual relationship is $\bd = \bd$.

Tone. There is an unfortunate belief that Renaissance music, especially sacred music, should be performed with a cool, "hooty" tone. This belief probably stems from the fact that boys' voices were originally used on the soprano part and the ensuing feeling that female sopranos should now eliminate all vibrato from their voices if they are to sing in pure Renaissance style. True, all the lines must be heard clearly and with very clean pitch; therefore, excessive vibrato cannot be tolerated. The conductor will need to choose the point at which the voices can deliver a clean, expressive line yet are not constricted. The dynamic level, which rarely rises very high, is an important consideration here. In general, the tone is governed by the message of the text. In all periods of choral music, *passus et sepultus est* and *et resurrexit tertia die* call for different projection of mood, but the construction of Renaissance music will not permit the extreme changes of tone and dynamics which are found later.

A belief also exists that Renaissance vocal music should be performed without instrumental accompaniment. Certain choirs, perhaps most notably the singers in the Sistine Chapel, did perform *a cappella,* but outside these isolated situations voices and instruments were combined in many different ways. The use of strings, woodwinds, and brass in unison with voices, if employed in a circumspect manner, can add immeasurably to the performance of Renaissance music. A double bass, contrabassoon, or bass clarinet doubling the bass part at an octave can help provide a solid foundation to a motet as well as steady the pitch. In a longer, sectionalized composition such as a mass, it is entirely appropriate to have an organ play an introduction and supply short interludes between the movements. The problems of falling pitch, which may occur during the course of a long work, are thereby eliminated.

Dynamics. It has already been mentioned that extremes in dynamics are inappropriate to the flowing Renaissance style. However, *subtle* crescendos and diminuendos are essential to the shaping of the phrases, the most important aspect of Renaissance music. A slight increase in the volume is usually called for in an ascending line; a descending line requires less. An imitative figure should be brought out so that it can be recognized, and suspensions should receive slight emphasis.

Speech. The text of Renaissance music is all-important, and the study of any composition from this period should begin with the words. In most cases, composers tried to create music that would enhance the text, so it is essential that conductors and singers know not only what the words are about in general, but also the meaning and correct pronunciation of each individual word. Only then can the proper emphasis be made within each phrase.

In the secular music of the Renaissance composers often used "word painting" in their music. The word *heaven* might utilize an upward-moving melody, while *earth* would be represented by downward motion. Grief and sadness might be depicted by augmented or diminished triads and a joyous attitude indicated by leaps in the melody. Performance of Renaissance madrigals makes great demands on the singers in regard to playing the role and believing what they are singing. More will be said on this subject under the third area of choral artistry.

The Baroque Period: 1600–1750

Rhythm. Possibly the most distinguishing characteristic of Baroque music is its powerful rhythmic thrust. During this period, metrical accent became more prominent. Baroque music, therefore, stands in sharp contrast to the flowing, irregularly accented lines of the Renaissance. The rising interest in opera created concern for the dramatic qualities of choral music. The rapid development of instrumental music and the proliferation of dance music, with its strong rhythmic patterns, provided composers with inspiration for new approaches to solo and ensemble singing.

Because of its strong rhythms, Baroque music is appealing to choral singers. Yet, there are pitfalls for groups who function without proper information regarding performance practices. It is true that some choral compositions of simple construction can be performed by large forces with impressive results, but, for the most part, Baroque music sounds best if sung by choirs of moderate size. Twenty-five to 30 good singers can present just about anything written by Bach or Handel. If the choir is made up of young singers with smaller voices, the number might be increased somewhat, but it is extremely difficult to produce the vital clarity and precision needed in Baroque music with more than 50 singers. A performance of Bach's *Mass in B Minor* by 300 singers and an orchestra of 70 players is simply not appropriate. Such monster shows are essentially a nineteenth-century concept of Baroque music and betray gross ignorance of the very points we are here discussing.

Another hazard in performing Baroque music is the tendency for conductors, in an attempt to create excitement, to overemphasize the metrical accent. By giving additional stress to the first beat of the measure (which will be heard anyway) the conductor may create a regularly recurring roadblock to the flow of the music. The composition then becomes "hung up" on every bar line and the vital thrust *through* the measure is destroyed. Sensing a loss of vitality, the worried conductor then begins to increase the tempo, trying to substitute speed for energy in the line. The result of this unwise approach to the creation of excitement is always disastrous. Baroque music must not feel hurried; the *flow* is the thing. Once it is set in motion, a sense of *inevitability of continuation* must persist. A fast tempo should be brisk, but never frenzied. The frequently heard, long rallentando at the end is also out of the style. A slight broadening at the last few notes preserves the excitement to the conclusion.

There exists a great deal of information regarding the execution of dotted rhythms in the Baroque period; I would urge extensive reading from the Bibliography on that point. Briefly, it should be said that whenever ♩. ♪ appears in Baroque music, the conductor must give it considerable thought, for its execution can vary considerably, ♩.. ♪ or ♩ ♪ (triplet) frequently being required.

Tone and dynamics.   These two aspects of choral music are closely related in the Baroque, and a rather wide range of each item is called for. A characteristic tone of Baroque music is that of voices and instruments together, not only in unison and octaves as in the Renaissance, but in many other relationships of accompaniment or equal partnership. In spite of those choirs that cling to the tradition of singing J. S. Bach's motets and chorales without instruments, *a cappella* music was quite rare in the Baroque period. Even when no instruments are mentioned in the score (as with five of the six motets of Bach), the music develops much more character when appropriate instruments are used on the vocal parts. For example, in the motet *Singet dem Herrn* (for double choir) a string ensemble of two violins, viola, and cello (possibly doubled by a string bass) might play with one choir while a contrasting color could be developed in the other choir by a quartet of two oboes and two bassoons. Lacking such extensive forces, the conductor could use two cellos, one on each bass part, and a harpsichord could fill in the harmony. Such combinations of voices and instruments are vastly more interesting to hear and clearly exemplify the Baroque concern for the concertato principle—contrast.

Even with the works that include instrumental parts, it is important to realize that Baroque composers were more interested in whether their music was performed than in what specific instruments were to play it. True, the solo instrument is usually indicated, but the bass line, for instance, might be played by a cello, a string bass, a bassoon, a contrabasson, a bass clarinet, or a combination of these instruments. Instrumentation should depend on the size and strength of the choir, the logistical arrangements, and the availability of players. A harpsichord or small organ can provide the harmony. The piano does not have an especially appropriate tone for this kind of work, but it is better to use that than nothing. In fact, the discreet doubling in octaves of a bass line can sound quite well on the piano.

The rugged character of Baroque music permits a wide range of vocal color and dynamics as well. In Handel's *Israel in Egypt,* the cries of those in bondage (first chorus) must contrast sharply with moments such as the sending of a great darkness over the land. Pianissimo and fortissimo are rare, but in the Baroque a movement was begun which would culminate 150 years later in the extreme demands of the Romantics. Crescendo and diminuendo are likely to be built into the music (terraced) by the addition and elimination of voices and instruments. Gradual, long swelling and fading of volume sound contrived in Baroque music.

Speech.   An important characteristic of the Baroque period was the development of the recitative, a device for the delivery of a large amount of text, often preceding the singing of a chorus or an aria. Most extended works from the Baroque require knowledgeable treatment of ornamentation and accompaniment of recitative.

The printed score originally included only the voice part and a figured bass line. Considerable study is necessary by the singer if the proper ornamentation is to be presented. Few modern editions of Baroque music include the appoggiaturas and other embellishments which were in common use. It is therefore necessary for the conductor to guide the soloist with reliable information which will promote the development of an artistic delivery.

The question of appropriate accompaniment to Baroque recitative is rather involved. For many years, the bass note and its realized harmony were fully sustained throughout the soloist's reciting; an organ was utilized when feasible. In the concert hall, a harpsichord and a cello were frequently substituted for the organ. More recent research indicates that many performers in Bach's time, and before, advocated a generally "short" style of recitative accompaniment—few, if any, chords were sustained. The solist delivered the message in a very free rhythm with virtually no possibility of being covered by the players. The chords served as a kind of simple punctuation.

To performers and audiences accustomed to the sustained style of recitative accompaniment, the short style may sound rather dry and perfunctory at first hearing. However, it is not difficult to adjust to the different sound, and the clearer delivery of the text more than compensates for anything missing from the instruments. Personally, I advocate an approach to the recitative that is in keeping with the general practice of Baroque performance—that of flexibility. Some chords should be cut short and others sustained for various lengths. It all depends on what best serves the music. In arriving at decisions of this nature, it is evident that conductors

must study extensively, experiment at the keyboard, listen to other performances, and, with the vital element of their own musical imagination, prepare a valid concept. Conductors *cannot* depend upon the soloists or the
organist (cellist and harpsichordist) to do this preparation; the conductor
alone is responsible.

It is hoped that these somewhat terse paragraphs on the style of
Renaissance and Baroque music have whetted the reader's appetite for
further study. The few items mentioned are rather general; yet curiously
enough they are frequently overlooked in performance today.

I would suggest that conductors begin their study of performance
practice with the following books: Thurston Dart's *The Interpretation of Music;*
Arthur Mendel's "Introduction" to *The Passion According to St. John: J. S.
Bach;* and Fritz Rothschild's *Stress and Movement in the Works of J. S. Bach.*
Subsequent study of the references marked in the Bibliography by an as-
terisk will yield tremendous benefits to the conductor who wishes to advance
the choir beyond the learned-note stage toward the goal of choral artistry.

SUBTLE FACTORS OF RHYTHM
AND DYNAMICS—PHRASING

At the heart of all fine performances of music is an enlightened understanding of phrasing, the process whereby a series of apparently unrelated notes
becomes a coherent musical idea. Without the performer's understanding
of how to strongly execute the phrases, any music will quickly become
monotonous; the ear and the musical mind tire of the lack of cohesion and
loss of sense of direction. Listening to unphrased or weakly phrased music is
very much like hearing a speaker who, in a voice devoid of interest, reads
straight on through commas, periods, and other marks of punctuation,
delivering clearly a stream of words, but no thoughts.

Failure to clarify for the listener the musical ideas in the score constitutes one of the most glaring weaknesses in choral music performance today.
Correctness of pitch, rhythm, and other techniques cannot compensate for
an absence of musical questions and answers, thoughts, and statements
which reveal to the listener the drama of the music. All music is essentially
dramatic. The building of tension toward climaxes and the subsequent
resolution of these points of conflict constitute a significant portion of the
emotional content of music. The artistic conductor must first perceive the
drama of the composition being directed and then make it apparent to
the performers through conducting technique and explanations. The units
from which one constructs the story or argument are the phrases.

As an example of a phrase that builds tension and resolves the conflict,
we can turn to a familiar hymn tune.

The first line contains a strong element of movement toward a climax. This feeling is created by the several repetitions of a single pitch (the active, dominant note of the key), the quick note of a different pitch, followed by a return to the repeated note pitch. The second line resolves the tension that has been created, by moving to a lower pitch, using no dotted rhythm, and concluding on the restful mediant tone of the key. If one continues through the hymn, one can easily feel the little dramas of progression to climax and resolution of conflict which occur from phrase to phrase. The composer has skillfully created this ebb and flow by using simple compositional techniques such as rising melodic lines, modulation, exact repetition, and restatement. This familiar melody is very simple, but it contains just the right combination of the obvious and the unexpected to give it memorable and lasting qualities. In short, it is a masterpiece in its own right. It has been enthusiastically sung for several generations and will undoubtedly stay around for a long time to come.

It is not always so easy to determine the phrases, their climaxes, and their tendency toward tension or resolution. In choral music, however, we have assistance with this problem, for the musical phrase usually coincides with the textual phrase. That is, the beginnings of sentences, together with commas, periods, and other punctuation marks, constitute fairly reliable guides to the beginnings and endings of musical ideas—phrases. The words may or may not indicate whether the phrase is building or receding, but frequently, especially in well-composed choral music, the words have provided the composer with inspiration which is skillfully reflected in the character of the musical phrases.

Having determined exactly where the phrase begins and ends, the conductor must see that the choristers start and finish *cleanly* together. If the first note of the phrase is sung to a word that begins with an explosive consonant or a vowel, there is little difficulty in getting a precise start.

You will remember from our discussion of speech technique that every beat or principal subdivision thereof must be marked by the sounding of a vowel or explosive consonant. It is obvious, then, that in beginning a phrase that starts with a pitch consonant it must be moved *ahead* of the beat.

Man   is   the   child   of   God.

The *m* of *man* must be intoned on the pitch G *ahead* of the beat so that the ă vowel will sound firmly *on* the beat.

Choruses seem to understand this need for starting cleanly together; if any part of their execution of phrases is well done, it will be the beginning part. Choirs do less well in bringing phrases to a convincing conclusion. The problem seems to lie in two distinct areas: (1) loss of breath with fading support, and (2) loss of concentration as the performers and conductor mentally prepare for the *next* phrase. Singers *must* realize that, once the phrase is begun, it must continue with unabating conviction to the *very end*, with the final bit of sound coming as precisely together as did the initial attack. Singers and players alike are often careless about the exact length of the final note in a phrase. Learning to take full breath in preparation for the attack and learning to control the expenditure of air so that there is an ample supply left to deliver the final notes of the phrase with assurance are basic components of learning to phrase properly. Singers and wind players are prone to take a quick breath just before the end of the phrase, thereby demolishing the line.

In the case of singing, there is often some difficulty in determining exactly where the final sound occurs. If the word ends with an explosive consonant, the problem is easier than if a vowel or tuned consonant concludes the final syllable. In the latter situation, the conductor must be prepared to explain and to show by means of conducting technique when the tuned consonant is made and exactly on what beat or subdivision the sound must cease. Additional uncertainty is created in the singers' minds when a breath has to be taken between phrases but no rests are indicated. Under no circumstances must the second phrase be late in starting; therefore, if breath must be taken, the time for this act must be taken from the end of the first phrase.

In this example from a Palestrina motet, no places for breath are apparent in the score. However, following the rules of speech, it is obvious that a break in the line is required after the vocative (*Regina coeli*) and at each comma. Although it may not be necessary to breathe at each of these points, it would be possible (depending on the tempo) to do so. Air could be taken in very quickly at the eighth rest created by shortening the last note of the phrase before. Particular care must be taken in starting the word *laetare*. The *l* must come before the beat so that the vowel *ae (eh)* will occur precisely on time. Otherwise the second phrase will feel late, and the forward impetus of the composition arrested.

It is important that, as the music moves from phrase to phrase, the character of the beginning of a phrase approximate that of the conclusion of the previous one. Because of the aforementioned problem of devitalization of the ends of phrases, an intake of breath before the start of the new phrase often rejuvenates a choir so strongly that their attack on the new phrase sounds like the start of a new composition or at least the declamatory arrival of reinforcements from an auxiliary choir! The singers must, therefore, learn to *meld* the phrases so that the listener is led smoothly and steadily through the music without disruption. This procedure is akin to the suggestion in Chapter 4 regarding the matching of vowel sounds (page 97). Releasing a phrase and picking up the next without disrupting the musical flow is also important to instrumental ensembles. When solo lines are passed from one instrument to another, say from flute to oboe, the oboist tries to pick up the character of the phrase as it was completed by the flutist. Careful attention to this technique of matching phrases will do much to ensure the continuity of the music.

The most important aspect of phrasing, however, is not to be found in precise attacks, releases, or matching character. These items can be handled with relative ease. What is most difficult to convey to singers (and players) is the powerful sense of forward motion or thrust that must permeate each musical statement. Without this impetus, the most correctly executed patterns of pitch, rhythm, tone, and dynamics become boring in the extreme. Music must always have the feeling of progressive movement if any sort of excitement or drama is to develop. It is vital that there always be a concern for *continuity* through the phrase, the movement, and the composition. The music must always *go on*. It is absolutely necessary to sing or play *through* the phrases. This unceasing, forward motion is what Mozart referred to when he said that music must flow like oil. It is what Toscanini was striving for with his constant battle cry of, "*Cantare! Sostenere!*" (Sing! Sustain!). It is the mark of every great performer. How can this vital point, so often lost even to trained musicians, be taught to choir singers?

First of all, the singers must be secure in their execution of active tone and legato. Restudy the exercises in Chapter 4 in the sections on Active Tone and Articulation. Without these technical accomplishments, a strong sense of *connectedness* will be impossible.

Next, there must be a clear understanding of what is generally referred to as "the *shape* of the phrase." All musical statements have a point of maximum interest—a climax. There may also be one or two minor peaks of interest in a phrase, but these are of less concern to us here. Conductors should establish in their own thinking as clearly as possible, the major point toward which the music is moving. The climax may be marked by a higher pitch, by a note of greater duration, or by metrical accent. Sometimes more than one of these factors will be apparent at the climax; rarely do all three occur simultaneously. In well-composed choral music, the important word or syllable of the text often occurs at the time of the musical climax.

This point of greatest interest may occur anywhere within the phrase but it typically falls near the middle, creating an arch-shaped melody.

It may also come near the end.

Occasionally it occurs at the very beginning, although this position is rare.

A problem may arise when one attempts to locate the climax, because musicians often disagree as to what constitutes the most important point. Certain conductors approach virtually all phrases as if they were arch-shaped. That is, the beginnings and endings are less intense; the maximum interest occurs in the middle. Other conductors stress the movement *through* the phrase so emphatically that every statement climaxes near the end. The whole subject is very personal and subtle. If conductors experiment and become secure in their own minds, they will then be able to direct with personal conviction.

At any rate, as the music moves toward the climax, a feeling of excitement must develop. The climax must be in proportion to what has led up to it; that is, the listeners must perceive the major point of interest, but their attention must not be unduly arrested by it unless a moment of tremendous emphasis is called for. After the climax, the music tapers off in its intensity, still retaining its vitality and forward movement.

Writings concerning phrasing usually mention this tension which should develop as the climax is approached and the relaxation which ensues as the phrase concludes. Choristers are often mystified by these terms *tension* and *relaxation*. Little wonder; they really have nothing to do with music. Tension and relaxation are not properties of sound. They may exist in the bodies (muscles) of the performers and, therefore, may be used for motivation, but they cannot be heard. Insofar as music performance is concerned, tension and relaxation are actually subtleties of dynamics and rhythm.

Mysterious as this may sound, I believe that as singers move to the climax of a phrase, they feel a growing tension, which is heard by the listener as a slight crescendo accompanied by a virtually imperceptible increase in the tempo. This quasi-accelerando feeling is created by what might be termed a "leaning" or pressing forward of the notes toward the point of greatest interest, a kind of "compression" of the beat. The phrase blooms on the climax and then tapers off as a slight diminuendo occurs and the pressing forward ceases as the beat is "stretched."

Now, before I am totally misunderstood on this important point, I would again point out that a critical aspect of artistic choral singing is sensitivity to subtle changes in pitch, dynamics, rhythm, and tone. A phrase must not be marred by gross swellings, rushings, blastings, subito pianos, and ritardandos, in that order. The artistically executed phrase may contain all those elements, but in a highly refined form. The finished product is the result of the conductor's artistic sensitivity which is transmitted or taught to the choir and is then reflected and demonstrated by them.

The techniques already mentioned on page 90 for the development of controlled crescendo and diminuendo should have laid a foundation for this approach to phrasing. The choir might then take some phrases and try building to the climax by deliberately exaggerating the crescendo and accelerando. The same procedure could be followed with diminuendo in completing the phrase. It will be found that it is difficult to control the diminuendo and at the same time to maintain interest, but, as with so many other points, the singers' *awareness* of the technical problem being studied governs the degree of successful accomplishment. It is scarcely possible to overemphasize the importance of teaching the choir members to shape their phrases with understanding and sensitivity, for in this action lies the basis of artistic music making. The building of tension or anticipation, followed by relaxation or fulfillment, is vital to holding the listener's attention. A continuous forte, piano, single color, or tempo can be deadly to the ears of an audience. Gradually, the choir will grow in its sensitivity. The singers will certainly realize that at this point there is no room for stumbles in pitch and rhythm or for other obtrusive technical factors which quickly destroy artistry.

Two factors constantly get in the way of sensitive phrasing: the text and the bar line.

If a study is made of the words of a composition (and this work should take place early in the rehearsal schedule), it will be immediately apparent that some words are more important than others. Nouns and verbs are usually key words. In the familiar text, "And the *glory,* the *glory* of the *Lord,* shall be *revealed,*" the italicized words carry the substance of the message. Speaking the words aloud will show where the emphasis should fall. However, when choristers begin to sing, there is a curious tendency to ignore the intrinsic importance of the key words and to hammer home every word or syllable with equal strength. The choir then is guilty of what I call "mono-inflection." The result is wearisome. No subtlety of phrasing can develop, and the music is rapidly beaten to death, the soprano part being the first to fall. This problem of mono-inflection is very apparent in hymn singing and other homophonic music. How often we hear the melody quoted at the beginning of this chapter thumped into a monotonous line by the one-level, deadening delivery of, "Onward, Christian soldiers, marching as to war"!

Directors who have poor conducting technique are likely to produce choirs that sing with mono-inflection. Awkwardly pointing out each word or syllable when it occurs rather than conducting the music almost always produces a monotonous regularity in both words and notes. Here again is pointed up the need for choral conductors who are well-grounded in their profession. Until a choir has become very alert to the sound of mono-inflection, a conductor will need to be constantly on guard against its appearance in rehearsals and performances. In good choral music, textual and musical emphasis regularly coincide, but when they do not (as in a translated text), the requirements of the musical lines must take precedence over the words.

The other factor that destroys phrasing is the bar line. It is obvious from the foregoing paragraphs that musical ideas are expressed in patterns of varying lengths and that accents are created by a variety of factors, only one of them being the metrical stress. If a strong beat occurs at regular intervals, it is apparent that attention will be drawn to that point and that the music will begin to form into measures rather than phrases. Very much as mono-inflection of the text destroys phrasing through the unrelenting hammering of identically emphasized words or syllables, so can the regularly recurring downbeat, unless handled with great care, create roadblocks in the flow of the lines.

Because of its position, the first note in a bar will receive a natural accent. Any additional stress given to the first beat may cause the music to stop or to feel heavy at that point. One of the most frequently encountered examples of this fault can be heard in beginning wind bands conducted by directors who beat with square patterns and a heavy hand. No buoyancy or flow can occur in music until an enlightened understanding of the function of the downbeat has taken place.

The first beat in the measure should be viewed as *a point of departure.* The music should immediately lift off this beat and move at once into the measure. The first beat, then, must have a buoyancy or lightness rather than weight. It might be considered as an energy station which regularly lifts the music *up,* not down.

Important as the first beat of each measure is, the key to the onward flow of the music is found not there, but rather in the so-called weak beat. Indeed, it is the latter part of the measure that is the crucial part. At that point it is essential to think *crescendo, energy, thrust,* or anything else necessary to propel the music over the bar line. The weak beat, the secret of strong phrasing, must become active in character.

Many conductors and choral singers do not understand this point. It is exactly contrary to the way we are often taught as children. When we first took music lessons, most of us were expected to emphasize the first beat of the measure. It is true that most of the music we hear today groups itself into units or measures of strong and weak pulses: S w S w in $\frac{2}{4}$ ("Joy to the World"), S w w S w w in $\frac{3}{4}$ ("Come Thou Almighty King"), and S w *medium* w, S w m w in $\frac{4}{4}$ ("Onward, Christian Soldiers"). A very delicate relationship exists among these pulses, and additional stress created by the performer can completely throw off the balance and destroy or weaken the flow of the music.

There is, of course, occasionally a need for strong accents in music. These spots arrest the attention of the listener and create excitement; without emphasis, music becomes bland. However, conductors must be aware that too many accents in succession (mono-inflection) or a regularly recurring stress (heavy downbeats) can kill the line of the music.

Conductors who are concerned for the vitality of their choir's sound would do well to study deeply these points concerning measures and how they relate to their conducting techniques. If the whole question is new to them, they can quickly get the point by playing some easy minuets of Bach, lightening the downbeat and moving the music strongly ahead at the last part of the measure. They might also experiment with their choirs, asking the members to sing a melody such as "America" with lifted downbeats and slight crescendo with thrust at the third beat. The buoyancy and vitality will be immediately apparent. The conductors may then ask themselves, "Does my conducting technique show this vitality and lift? Do I cause my ensemble to soar or to plod?" The following statements may then provide the maestro with specific points for study.

1. The downbeat must not be too heavy. Except when strong emphasis is required, the downbeat must suggest "lift off."
2. The so-called weak beats in the pattern must show energy and thrust.
3. Music can withstand only a few consecutive identically emphasized beats. Do not cause mono-inflection by conducting with a "one-beat" pattern. Mirroring the pattern of the right hand with the left, or other ungainly motions, may compound the tendency to thump the music.
4. It is important not to give heavy stress to a long-held and/or high note. Such an emphasis will create a double or triple accent, which may demolish the line.
5. Furthermore, do not hit *any* note so strongly that expansion of the note is impossible. It is vital that all notes "bloom." Listen critically to various choral groups to hear if a decrescendo is made on every note. This weakness is very common.
6. Do not change $\frac{4}{4}$ into $\frac{2}{4}$ by making the third beat in $\frac{4}{4}$ as strong as the first. The third beat in $\frac{4}{4}$ is stronger than two or four, but weaker than one. This subtlety is frequently overlooked.
7. $\frac{6}{8}$ is not made up of two measures of $\frac{3}{4}$ or $\frac{3}{8}$. The fourth beat in $\frac{6}{8}$ is not as strong as the first. If $\frac{6}{8}$ needs to be conducted in 2, the second beat is not as strong as the first. Throw away your editions of "Silent Night" that have been set in $\frac{3}{4}$.
8. Be alert to the rhythmic excitement inherent in dotted rhythms. ♩. ♪ and ♩. ♪ frequently require a slight break at the dot to permit the short note to sound clearly and energetically. At this break, the vitality of the rhythm is intensified; my term for this technique is "renewal." Do not neglect the little notes in dotted rhythms or elsewhere.
9. A similar opportunity for renewal is often available at tied notes. Try substituting an intensely felt rest for the tied note; the break may be just what is needed to clarify the rhythm.
10. Of all the motions the conductor makes, the *preparatory* beat is undoubtedly the most important. Within it lies not only the tempo but also the dynamics, tone, and general character of everything that is to follow. Study your preparatory beat. Make it say everything possible. It is like the poised moment before a champion diver springs. Teach your choir to prepare and *to continue to prepare* before each entrance.

CHORAL ARTISTRY AND THE THEATER

Both conductors and singers can learn a great deal about enhanced performance of music from discussion with theatrical directors and from observation of and participation in various aspects of dramatic productions. Choral music and theater are much more closely related than many choral conductors realize. The truly great choirs exemplify most of the characteristics that will be mentioned in this section.

It is possible to discern three distinct categories of information pertaining to this subject. First, the actor has many techniques that can help the conductor (and therefore the singers) arrive at an interpretation of a choral composition. Second, the singer can learn much from the actor about how to present a convincing performance. Finally, in live performances of choral music, the theater has many resources which can assist a choir in producing a visually attractive, artistic entity. Let us consider these three categories in that order.

Acting Techniques for
Conductors and Singers

When an actor is preparing a role, a routine is carried out which in many ways parallels the series of techniques we have discussed for choral music. He reads the part aloud to develop correct pronunciation and clear articulation; he calls upon a knowledge of the voice to develop fullness of projection; he thinks through possible gestures and bodily movements and practices them.

The actor, however, is likely to be much more concerned than the singer with what might be called the *motivation*. What is happening in the play that necessitates a particular tone or dynamic level in the voice? Why is a certain movement necessary at a particular moment? Is there a uniformity of motivation among all of the players on stage in a specific scene? The actor-singer, as in musicals or opera, understands this need for motivation; without it, no drama takes place. The solo singer, it is hoped, also looks for the motivation in developing an interpretation of songs; without it, we hear little more than pleasant tone and correct notes. The choral singer is much less likely to look for the meaning or motivation. I believe that this is the primary reason that choral music in performance so often lacks conviction. There is little or no thought to motivate the techniques, and therefore the music does not develop.

Conductors are aware, of course, that their singers need to be "inspired." The rehearsals may include an explanation of the text or even a dramatic reading of the words, but this process usually does not go far enough. It seems to me that only in a handful of truly fine choruses does one hear a sense of deep, personal involvement by the singers in the *drama* of the composition. It is the conductor's responsibility to see that the singers know how to develop this involvement. It is not enough for the conductor alone to be inspired or motivated, although the director's emotional involvement may very well spread to the choir; indeed, this is an important first step. Far more can happen, however, if all the choir members are motivated. It cannot be overstressed that each chorister must develop an *inner motivation*. Merely observing a printed *ff* on the page or a ferocious gesture from the conductor will not provide true motivation. The performers must constantly ask themselves, "Why?" The conductor can assist the singers in motivation by teaching them something about dramatics. Let us, therefore, look at some very simple principles of acting and see how they may be applied to choral singing.

We have probably all experienced the irritating, painful, exasperating event of stubbing a bare toe on a piece of furniture. This event may have taken place at two o'clock in the morning as we were awakened and went to answer the insistent ringing of the telephone which turned out to be a wrong number! Upon our impact with the chair leg, our reaction would be fully revealed to anyone who might observe us. There would be an immediate tenseness throughout the body, possibly a clutching for the injured toe. The face would contort, and there would be an exclamation which would vary according to the severity of the pain. Your customary, normal way of expressing yourself vocally would come to the fore and show itself as a sharp intake of breath, a mumbled exclamation, or a stream of profanity. Now keep in mind these three factors through which an inner motivation is outwardly manifested—the body, the face, and the voice. These are the three items which an actor uses to play the event of hitting one's toe on a chair. The actor's body, face, and voice are the instruments through which the audience is reached. It is also through the body, the face, and the voice that a singer expresses the meaning of the music that is inwardly felt.

Let us now suppose that an actor or actress is required to play a scene such as we have just described. As she comes in contact with the chair leg, she attempts to convince the audience that she has hurt her toe. She tenses her body, screws up her face, and utters a cry. However, the audience will not believe her unless the three actions are *motivated;* without motivation, the actress will only appear as a person *pretending* to have stubbed her toe. Is it necessary, therefore, for the actress, night after night, to actually drive her foot into the chair leg in order to achieve motivation for her reactions? Hopefully, no. If it were necessary, we would then have that most unfortunate situation, decried by G. B. Shaw, of an actor *living* the part. What the actress must do instead, is *believe* that she has hit her foot. Then, according to the depth and sincerity of her belief, will the outward manifestation take on an air of conviction and truth. The audience will then also believe the event. The basis of acting, therefore, is believing.[1]

In developing their acting skills, players work to increase their ability to believe in depth the various roles they are called upon to play. They are assisted in this growth by recall of their own life experiences—the first attempt to smoke, a quarrel with a bitter enemy, the receiving of unexpected good news, the death of a loved one. Recalling these events enables an actor to reconstruct the scene mentally and emotionally, to believe that he or she is actually in the scene, and to motivate the outward expressions in a convinc-

---

[1]Charles McGaw, *Acting Is Believing* (New York: Holt, Rinehart and Winston, Inc., 1955). I strongly recommend study of this book for further elaborations on this point.

ing manner. As actors grow older, their life experience provides them with more and more material for recall.

Actors, of course, need not personally experience every characterization they are called upon to portray. It is not necessary or desirable to have experienced paralysis in order to play a person in a wheelchair, or to have been beaten up in a fight to enact such a scene. One can observe, study, and converse with streetwalkers, blind men, 90-year-old matriarchs, police officers, absent-minded professors, and innumerable other characters whose portrayal might be required on stage. Actors are indeed keen observers of mankind. It is from these deep studies of other people that powerful motivations are often developed.

Yet, even more important than recall of one's own life experiences or the observations of other people and events is the actor's ability to imagine or to fantasize. We all have our reveries, and it is in these great escapes from day-to-day tedium that an actor frequently finds the basis for motivation. Fantasies, of course, are often developed from one's own life experiences or observations, but no person alive today was present at the signing of the Declaration of Independence, the building of the pyramids, or the crucifixion of Jesus of Nazareth. An actor can study the event, sometimes in considerable detail, but eventually he must fantasize the situation to the point where he *believes* he is present. Then, his outward actions (body, face, voice) convey his beliefs with sincerity and he is able to present a convincing characterization to an audience. A perfect example of this deep belief can be observed in children's play. A group of small boys pushing their toy trucks through roads and mountain passes in a sandpile, at the same time uttering motor-like sounds of straining engines, are not pretending. They are in earnest; they believe; their performance is convincing.

Three factors, then, recall of personal life experiences, observation of others' experiences, and fantasy or imagination, combine in various ways to provide an actor with motivation. A great actor or actress believes, and the audience believes. She does not *pretend,* and she certainly does not *live* the part. The key word is *belief.*

Presenting a Convincing Performance

The opera singer develops a role by drawing upon exactly these same resources. All the musical preparations are made, melodies and words are memorized, costumes and makeup are put on. The success of a role, however, depends upon the depth of the characterization, which, unfortunately, is sometimes rather shallow. Opera productions may be little more than concerts in costume, although things are now better in this regard than they were a generation ago. Training in opera now includes considerable work in acting.

The solo singer in recital also must believe. The musical problems need to be carefully worked out, but the success of the singer depends almost entirely upon an ability to project the message and to convince the audience. We have all heard recitalists give stunning performances when the voice was really not at its best or even when it had aged well beyond its prime. I recall an overwhelming Wagnerian performance by a Wotan who had long before passed the peak of his vocal powers. One was scarcely aware of the technical deficiencies, so great was the artistry. There was no problem in believing the characterization.

The choir singer may not understand this need to search for a motivation. Because the members of a choir usually have far less training than solo singers, a great portion of rehearsal time is devoted to perfecting intonation, rhythm, phrasing, and other musical matters. Feeling a certain comfort in the fact that he is but one of a considerable number of basses, the individual bass singer may not grasp the importance of seeking the drama in the choral work he is singing. As he normally wears no costumes or makeup and is restricted to a considerable extent in his bodily movement, he may have difficulty thinking of himself as an actor. He devotes most of his attention to singing the correct notes and leaves the spotlight to the conductor.

In so withdrawing, this choir singer detracts immeasurably from the performance. Not realizing that it is *his* face, rather than the conductor's, that is seen by the audience, he delivers his notes with an absolutely blank expression, betraying a total lack of inner involvement. Having given little thought to what he is singing about, no motivation is developed, and no stimuli are fed to the body, face, or the voice. The performance then becomes sterile, both visually and aurally. The greatest damage is done to the choir, when the *sound* is unmotivated.

The human voice is a most flexible, expressive, and glorious musical instrument. It is capable of delivering an infinite number of tone colors, reflecting the full range of human emotions. The voice is sensitive beyond belief to motivation; the slightest changes in thought are immediately apparent in the sound of the voice. Absence of thought produces absence of color, all too common in choral singing. A choir may have developed a pleasant, free-flowing tone, free from strain and other vocal problems, but if it does not truthfully convey the emotional message of the composition being performed, no beauty of sound can compensate for the lack of "dramatic integrity" in the tone. Development of truth in the tone may well be the single most important factor in choral music. It is very interesting to note that actors who sing (sometimes not very well) are invariably more successful in their character portrayals in musical productions than trained singers who have never learned to act.

Let us now consider how some of these basic principles of dramatization may be taught to a choir. Suppose the composition being rehearsed is Randall Thompson's "The Pasture"; the text is by Robert Frost. Once the notes and other technical considerations are in order, the choir might be urged to construct mentally the scene of the poem. As is common in Frost's writings, some unnamed, unseen person is being addressed:

I'm going out to clean the pasture spring;
I'll only stop to rake the leaves away
(And wait to watch the water clear, I may):
I sha'n't be gone long.—You come too.[2]

It is probable that but two people are involved. There is between these people the tenderest of relationships, although few words of endearment are spoken. There is a great feeling of shared joy of simple events, a quiet contemplation of a pastoral scene. Drawing upon their own past experiences, observations, or fantasies, the members of the choir must develop their motivation. They may place themselves in the scene or be on the sidelines as silent, unseen observers. They must develop the setting—the spring, the path, a stream, hills, trees. Most important, they must visualize the couple and work to develop in themselves the feeling that exists between these two people, who may be boyfriend and girlfriend, husband and wife (of any age), grandfather and grandchild, or any other couple to whom the singer can relate. It does not work for the conductor to set up the scene, name the characters, and tell everyone to imagine it. Such a procedure may arrest the development of the individual's thoughts. Success in this activity depends almost entirely upon the ability of the conductor to generate a creative atmosphere which encourages the singers to develop their own inner motivation in detail. When the motivation is deep and personal, the outward manifestation will be true: the body, although remaining stationary, will suggest the tranquility of the situation; the face will reflect the serenity of the inner thinking; the voice will produce a tone of love, tenderness, and quiet joy, all these factors being motivated at a highly personal, individual level. When the choir members project this kind of thought, they have transcended the technique of choral music and have begun to perform artistically.

It is not always so easy to develop the mental picture as it was with "The Pasture." Especially with younger singers lacking life experiences, the conductor must be prepared to furnish material for the singers which will assist them with their motivation. I remember once working with a choir to establish a feeling of conviction in the "Dies Irae" from Mozart's *Requiem*. Although the notes were correct, the feeling of a day of wrath was totally absent. I then recalled two events from my own life which I related in some detail to the choir. One concerned a time when I was lost on a mountain top, above tree line, in a severe electrical storm. I described as vividly as I could the driving rain, the sizzling of lightning around me, the almost constant roar of thunder. I also told the choir of the night when my home town in Maine was leveled by a great forest fire. Although it was more than 30 years before, I clearly remembered the awful walls of flame fanned by 100-mile-an-hour winds, giant trees turned into flaming torches, and above all, the unearthly sound. I was able to convince the choir that I had some concept of what a *dies irae* might include. I do not know what section of my narration fired the fantasies of my singers, but the rendition of the music that we gave a few minutes later left us all emotionally exhausted, so great was the feeling of terror that was unleashed. I closed the rehearsal at that point, and the singers, with scarcely a word, literally staggered out of the room. They, too, had gained a grasp of what the great sequence *Dies Irae* was about.

It is especially important when the choir is singing in a foreign language that the conductor give a clear explanation of the text and that the singers find their personal relationship to it. For example, consider in Bruckner's *Locus Iste,* the phrase,

Locus iste a Deo factus est
(Here is a place made by God)

In a text such as this, the conductor must be aware that "a place made by God" means many things to many people. It *may* be in a great cathedral with flickering candles, stained glass windows, and the like. But to some people a place made by God, a place of great beauty and holiness, would be at a wind-swept moor, on a rocky seacoast, or within a forest of giant redwood trees. It might also be, to some people, backstage at a concert hall, or to others, in the intimate embrace of a loved one. It makes no difference. The important thing is that *all* the singers must work diligently to find the place most meaningful to them, to project themselves into it, and to believe. The rest will follow naturally.

When a choir first begins to work on this inner motivation, the conductor may find that some singers experience difficulty in freeing themselves from long-established inhibitions or repressions. They may find it very upsetting to permit inner thoughts to be made apparent. They may also feel that such involvement is inappropriate for choral performance.

To convince and assist these hesitant ones, the conductor might try utilizing a small group from the choir to demonstrate the principle. For example, I was once working to obtain a greater sense of the drama in the chorus *Lasset uns den nicht zerteilen* ("Do not rend it or divide it") from J. S. Bach's *Passion According to St. John.* I was trying to obtain from the choir the great contrast that occurs when the Roman soldiers, having crucified Jesus, turn their attention to dividing up his garments, finally casting lots for his coat. I wanted the atmosphere of worldliness and bickering to be clearly apparent over the agitated bass line. After several failures, I selected a quartet of my more adventuresome singers and asked them to perform before the choir. They actually moved about and sang to one another, believing their role as soldiers. I gradually added more singers to the small ensemble, bringing it up to about twelve. After several repetitions, the demonstration group really got involved in the act, singing with buoyancy and verve. Some were actually on their knees examining garments and throwing dice. Some stood apart, disdainfully leaning on their spears. My wishes for the composition were then clearly apparent to the choir; when the selected group was returned to the main body of singers, the entire group believed their role. Too operatic? Possibly. Dramatic? Most certainly. Is not all music dramatic?

This same technique might be applied to a composition such as "Make Believe," from Jerome Kern's *Showboat.* Try starting the demonstration with a couple. Let them sing to each other, hold hands, stroll about. Pair off the entire choir and station them around the room. Have everyone walk casually in place. Let the choir members return to their customary places and each visualize the person to whom he or she has been singing. The tone and facial expression should have become ideal.

If this dramatic aspect of choral music is to be developed fully in the choir, the conductor and singers must be aware of several factors that will influence the degree of success. First of all, this creative atmosphere is an illusion that is easily shattered. The singers must learn that not only must they develop their own motivation, but also they must assist their colleagues to motivate. The utmost respect must be held for each other's growth. Singers must particularly guard against stepping out of character. A careless, unmotivated body movement or facial expression (grimace, smirk, and so on) destroys the illusion. So does looking at the audience, or taking more than a quick glance at the printed music. The choristers must know that singers in the ensemble who are not believing what they are singing are as conspicuous to everyone present as if they were clad in white sports clothes in the midst of strictly formal attire. This last point can be easily proven at almost any choir concert; the nonbelievers will be apparent to all.

Second, the music must be *thoroughly* learned. A singer with his or her head in the score can contribute nothing; indeed, that singer detracts. There is much to be said for singing without the printed music in hand. Only then can complete manifestations of inner belief be made. Memorizing requires a great deal of time, however. It might be better to study more music. Also, memorizing, unless thorough, may cause technical weaknesses which mar the artistry. It is best for the printed score to be retained in the singer's hands and reduced to a position where it is needed for occasional reference only. Even in extended choral works, where memorizing is not practical, the singers must learn the music so well that an occasional quick glance at the score suffices to keep them on the track. My rule is: One glance per line! Choral singers must deal with themselves severely on this point. In too many choirs one encounters the situation where the singers only occasionally peek at the conductor, never at crucial moments!

Third, the singers must have room to move. Choir members cannot develop full potential when packed onto risers shoulder to shoulder with little room to breathe. Except with special compositions requiring the singers to move from place to place, there is no need to stroll around; they must, however, have room for a limited amount of axial movement. Only with this freedom can the body deliver its response to the motivation.

Finally, a word of caution regarding overemoting. There is, in all performer-audience relationships, an inherent need for exaggeration, an exhibitionism or largeness of expression which carries the emotion to the remote corners of the auditorium. Determining the degree of projection required is not easy. One does not normally speak or gesticulate in a telephone booth in the same manner as when addressing a group in a large hall. There must be constant concern for reaching the audience, and at the same time the conductor and singer must both guard against their personal, emotional involvement throwing everything out of control. I have already mentioned the undesirability of an actor's *living* the part. The same point holds true for the conductor and the chorister. As the ability to believe deeply, to motivate, and to manifest grows, there is a distinct danger of the carefully rehearsed techniques falling to pieces. Excessive exuberance, coupled with feeble technique, is the mark of a dilettante or poor musician. Always, but especially at moments of high emotional fervor, there must be a portion of the intellect that remains coolly objective and ever alert to fluctuating pitch or rhythm, to faulty diction, to unbalanced dynamics, and to unpleasant tone. Maintaining balance between technique and artistry may well be the greatest problem in all performance of music.

Admittedly, it is far easier to develop this sense of drama in compositions that are interpretive, subjective, or Romantic. However, this difficulty is never an excuse for performing with blank minds, faces, and voices. There must be constant work to find the meaning and emotional expression. In seeking a motivation for performance of more objective texts such as *Magnificat anima mea Dominum* ("My soul doth magnify the Lord") or *Ecce, ancilla Domine fiat mihi secundum verbum tuum* ("Behold the handmaid of the Lord; be it unto me according to thy word"), someone is nevertheless speaking in a definite setting. Although the message may be less dramatic than other texts we have considered in this discussion, it is still possible, through study and research, to learn the background of the words and to expound them with depth. It does not do to rely upon a mere projection of mood. Indeed, no music or text exists that is best performed by an expressionless or impersonal style; such compositions would truly be by and for automatons.

Development of Deep Belief and Lucid Manifestation

The following list, a summary of points considered in the first two categories of Choral Artistry and the Theater, will provide the singers with definite steps to take as they develop depth of belief and manifestation.

Follow the sequence carefully; note that certain key items are regularly repeated.

1.   Read the words aloud. Make sure the reading is neither nonintelligent nor nondramatic, flaws often present in performing works with foreign text.
2.   Allow time for the drama to come to full bloom in your imagination. Avoid the fallacy of attempting to learn a composition in one rehearsal.
3.   For a time, assume that the composer was somehow inspired to present a picture. Seek to find that picture.
4.   By means of your life experiences, your observations, and your imagination, develop and *maintain* the picture in your mind. Constantly explore your inner self to find ways in which you can relate to the drama. Feed your imagination.
5.   The conductor can suggest pictures, but must not outline a specific scene for everyone to utilize.
6.   Put yourself in the picture.
7.   The *depth, detail,* and *constancy* of your picture determine its success.
8.   If you do not show your face almost all the time, the picture of your involvement is destroyed. A few seconds of your face in your score kills the image. Look up!
9.   If the conductor is too vigorous, the picture may be destroyed. Excessive movements can detract the audience's attention from the drama that shows on the faces of the singers.
10. Free yourself from the score. Memorize to the point where one glance per line is all that is needed.
11. Study your picture until you can personally relate to it and believe it.
12. Believe what you are singing, and work to make others believe.
13. A singer who is not believing will express little feeling regardless of a fine technique. Any doubt expressed by a singer can upset the belief of others, singers and audience alike.
14. Sustain your belief. Constantly renew your mental picture. Strengthen your inner vision.
15. You must be interested and involved (believing). Listeners are not likely to be interested in what does not interest the singer.
16. Choristers must learn to involve themselves physically in their singing; utilize the face, the eyes, the body.
17. A physical response to the music is an important way of projecting the emotion. Learn to take a breath in the style of the phrase that follows.
18. Sing with your eyes.
19. Practice projecting facial expression. Mirror the conductor's countenance. If you have trouble doing this at first, smile. It will give your face something to do temporarily. Never sing with a blank expression.
20. Learn to sing in your mind—in your imagination.
21. At times, the choir should sing silently, inwardly. Show strong eye and facial expression.
22. Sing in the mind up to a predetermined point (possibly a cadence), then aloud. This procedure is a good test of the choir's ability to *think* clean pitch.
23. Our thoughts seem to have as much effect on our voice as actions we actually take. Think deeply about the text and the music. Believe.

24. When you sing (for example) *Kyrie eleison,* do not *pretend* you are asking God for mercy. You must *believe* that is what you are doing.
25. You will know when you have been successful in believing.
26. The key to a truthful interpretation lies within you, not in the score.
27. You must not fear to become personally involved in the drama. Do not be afraid to rejoice, extol, lament, suffer, and so on.
28. The relationship between the singers and the conductor should be one of constant, reciprocal permeation, elucidation, and inspiration. Unceasingly work to infect one another with the drama.
29. Again, read the text aloud. Ask, has the drama matured and become apparent?
30. The eventual goal is crystalline externalization of truthfully conceived, inner motivation.

Technical Assistance for Effective Presentations

The theater itself, from the technical standpoint, can supply much assistance to the choir in search of enhanced performances. Conductors must face the fact that audiences today, through the influence of television, have become highly oriented toward the visual. The public expects color, movement, continuity, "pizazz," if you will. Frankly, the average choir concert is not very exciting from these standpoints. The problem is not so difficult for a band or orchestra, where there is always a certain amount of movement in the manipulation of the instruments, plus a variety of glittering highlights from polished woods and metals.

There is currently a rising interest in the "show choir," which dances and acts, and in compositions that call for synchronized body movements, lighting changes, and other extra-musical factors. Show choirs are a special situation, beyond our concerns here, but the more traditional choir can learn much from observing them.

To begin with, a choir should have an attractive, uniform appearance. There are many routes that can be taken in this regard. Most simply, men can wear dark suits and identical shirts and ties. Women can wear black skirts and white blouses. This basic plan can be extended to include dinner jackets for the men and more formal dresses for the women. Young choirs can wear dark pants and skirts and white shirts and blouses; a church choir usually wears gowns. Uniformity is the important thing. As we are trying to create an attractive picture, any distracting element such as glittering jewelry, extreme hair styles, or exotic footgear should be eschewed.

The conductor should be very conscious of his or her appearance from the rear. A suit jacket should be correctly cut so that, when the conductor's arms are raised, the collar does not bunch up at the neck. Especially distracting to the audience is the center pleat on the conductor's coat which sometimes snaps open and shut with a scissor-like precision, revealing at each gap an expanse of posterior anatomy and rumpled shirttail. There is much to be said for the men wearing the traditional formal, full-dress suit; women usually look best on the podium when wearing a long gown.

Altogether, it is scarcely possible to give too much attention to the appearance of the choir. It might be well to have someone with an eye for details present at the dress rehearsal to check points of appearance which might have been overlooked by the conductor or manager.

Of equal importance to the visual aspects of the concert is the stage setting and the lighting. The choir must be placed so that at least the face of every singer can be clearly seen. If the choir has plenty of room, proper spacing of the singers on risers will permit more of the body to be seen. Do not hide the choir behind a grand piano! When this is done, a great deal of communication is cut off between the conductor and performers, and between the choir and the audience.

Careful consideration should be given to the lighting of the entire choral scene as viewed from the audience. The singers' faces should appear neither garishly white nor artificially colored. If the choir performs before an acoustical shell, consider lighting it from below to avoid distracting shadows falling on it. A subtle blending of colored lights on the shell can add warmth to the total scene. If the risers and shell are set on a theater stage, the cyclorama might be lighted to enhance the total picture. You might even at times consider projections of stained glass windows, gothic arches, or simple patterns of variegated color on the cyclorama to create illusions that might enhance the audience's enjoyment of the music. It is often effective to change the lighting at some point in the program.

Attention must be given to the flow or continuity of the production. Once in motion, the concert must carry the audience forward with unabating firmness. Unless the entire program is devoted to a single large work, choral concerts are usually made up of many short compositions. The conductor must arrange these pieces so that they follow one another in a logical pattern, providing continuity and, simultaneously, variety. It is often effective to connect several short compositions with instrumental interludes of an improvisatory character. The continuity of a concert or section of a program is frequently broken by tardy performers, misplaced music, lackadaisical taking of places on stage, temperamental conductors who like to keep the audience waiting, applause in the wrong places, excessive and unnecessary tuning of instruments, adjustment of music stands, rearrangement of performers between compositions, pompous and irrelevant speeches by the conductor, and so on. Performers in the theater seem to be much more alert to the problems of flow than are musicians. An experienced stage manager should be available to handle the entire *mise en scene*. Concerts have succeeded or failed on the execution of details which are sometimes contemptuously dismissed as extra-musical but which, in reality, are essential components of the artistic whole. A fine performance is theatrically effective as well as technically correct and truthfully motivated.

CONCLUSION

With a full knowledge of his or her personal capabilities and limitations, of vocal technique, choral technique, and choral artistry, the maestro should now be prepared to pilot the choir on a firm course toward sublime choral performance. On the first part of the journey there must be a judicious blending of vocal training and repertoire; the work of Chapters 3 and 4 must go hand in hand; the study of voice and rehearsal of repertoire complement each other. Excessive attention to vocal technique without immediate application to compositions will cause loss of enthusiasm; plunging into note-learning procedures without knowing how to sing will eventually bring a choir to the brink of disaster. Maintain a balance between vocal and choral techniques. Remember—posture, breathing, support, freedom, resonance, and pitch, rhythm, tone, dynamics, text. Rotate your corrections and rehearsings among these ten items as necessary. Do not assume your choristers can all sing beautifully, but if they can, why waste time teaching what is already known? Do not labor isolated points.

Similarly, if your choir is a long-established, knowledgeable choral body, move as rapidly as possible to working on choral artistry (Chapter 5). Experienced, erudite choristers who are accustomed to working together usually prefer to begin dealing with interpretive matters at once. Minor problems of choral technique will usually clear up as the professional choir advances artistically. Almost any chorus of stable membership under the direction of a good conductor can, within a few years, achieve this level of competence. It is to achieving this end that this book is directed.

BIBLIOGRAPHY

Conducting Technique

ADLER, SAMUEL. *Choral Conducting: An Anthology.* New York: Holt, Rinehart and Winston, 1971.

BOULT, ADRIAN CEDRIC. *A Handbook on the Technique of Conducting,* new ed. Oxford: Hall, 1943.

GREEN, ELIZABETH A. H. *The Modern Conductor,* 2nd ed. Englewood Cliffs, N.J.: Prentice-Hall, Inc., 1969.

HABERLEN, JOHN. *Mastering Conducting Techniques.* Champaign, Ill.: Mark Foster Music Company, 1977.

HOLMES, MALCOLM. *Conducting an Amateur Orchestra.* Cambridge, Mass.: Harvard University Press, 1951.

MCELHERAN, BROCK. *Conducting Technique.* New York: Oxford University Press, 1966.

MCKELVY, JAMES. *Music for Conducting Class.* Champaign, Ill.: Mark Foster Music Company, 1977.

MOE, DANIEL. *Problems in Conducting,* rev. ed. Minneapolis: Augsburg Publishing House, 1973.

SCHERCHEN, HERMANN. *Handbook of Conducting.* Trans. M. D. Calvocoressi. London: Oxford University Press, 1933.

Vocal Production, Singing Technique, and Class Voice

BAKER, GEORGE. *The Common Sense of Singing.* New York: The Macmillan Company, 1963.

BEHNKE, EMIL, and CHARLES W. PEARCE. *Thirty Voice-Training Exercises.* New York: G. Schirmer, Inc., n.d.

BOWEN, GEORGE OSCAR, and KENNETH C. MOOK. *Song and Speech.* Boston: Ginn and Company, 1952.

BURGIN, JOHN CARROLL. *Teaching Singing.* Metuchen, N.J.: The Scarecrow Press, Inc., 1973.

BURTON, KURTH L. *Sensitive Singing.* Oakville, Ont., Canada: Leslie Music Supply, 1973.

CARROLL, CHRISTINA. *Improving Voice Training Techniques.* Tempe: Arizona State University Press, 1972.

CHRISTY, VAN A. *Expressive Singing, Vols. I and II.* Dubuque, Iowa: William C. Brown, Co., Publishers, 1961.

————. *Foundations in Singing.* Dubuque, Iowa: William C. Brown Co., Publishers, 1965.

CLIPPINGER, D.A. *The Clippinger Class–method of Voice Culture.* Bryn Mawr, Penn.: Oliver Ditson Company, 1933.

CONCONE GIUSEPPE. *Fifty Lessons for the Voice, Op. 9.* New York: G. Schirmer, Inc., n.d.

HELLIER, MARJORIE. *How to Develop a Better Speaking Voice.* Hollywood: Wilshire Book Company, 1959.

KAGEN, SERGIUS. *On Studying Singing.* New York: Dover Publications, Inc., 1950.

KLEIN, JOSEPH J., and OLE A. SCHJEIDE. *Singing Technique.* Tustin, Calif.: National Music Publishers, 1972.

LAMPERTI, G. B. *Techniques of Bel Canto.* New York: G. Schirmer, Inc., 1905.

————. *Vocal Wisdom.* Recorded and explained by William Earl Brown. New York: Hudson Offset Company, Inc., 1931.

LAWSON, JAMES TERRY. *Full-Throated Ease: A Concise Guide to Easy Singing.* Vancouver: Western Music Co., 1955.

LEHMANN, LILLI. *How to Sing.* Trans. from German by Richard Aldrich. New York: The Macmillan Company, 1924.

MILLER, RICHARD. *English, French, German and Italian Techniques of Singing.* Metuchen, N.J.: The Scarecrow Press, Inc., 1977.

NORDICA, LILLIAN. "Hints to Singers," in *Yankee Diva: Lillian Nordica and the Golden Days of Opera* by Ira Glackens. New York: Coleridge Press, 1963.

PUNT, NORMAN A. *The Singer's and Actor's Throat.* London: William Heinemann Medical Books, Limited, 1967.

ROMA, LISA. *The Science and Art of Singing.* New York: G. Schirmer, Inc., 1956.

ROSEWALL, RICHARD B. *Handbook of Singing.* Evanston, Ill.: Summy-Birchard Company, 1961.

SCHIØTZ, AKSEL. *The Singer and His Art.* London: Hamish Hamilton, 1970.

SHAKESPEARE, WILLIAM. *The Art of Singing.* Bryn Mawr, Penn.: Oliver Ditson Company, 1921.

TKACH, PETER. *Vocal Artistry.* Park Ridge, Ill.: Kjos Music Co., 1950.

————. *Vocal Technique.* Park Ridge, Ill.: Kjos Music Co., 1948.

TRUSLER, IVAN, and WALTER EHRET. *Functional Lessons in Singing.* Englewood Cliffs, N.J.: Prentice-Hall, Inc., 1972.

VACCAI, NICCOLO. *Practical Italian Vocal Method.* New York: G. Schirmer, Inc., 1923.

VENNARD, WILLIAM. *Singing: The Mechanism and the Technic.* New York: Carl Fischer, Inc., 1967.

WESTERMAN, KENNETH N. *Emergent Voice.* Ann Arbor, Mich.: Edwards Brothers, Inc., 1947.

Phonetics, Diction, and Translation

ADLER, KURT. *Phonetics and Diction in Singing: Italian, French, Spanish, German.* Minneapolis: University of Minnesota Press, 1967.

COX, RICHARD G. *The Singer's Manual of German and French Diction.* New York: G. Schirmer, Inc., 1970.

DENES, PETER B., and ELLIOT N. PINSON. *The Speech Chain.* Baltimore: Waverly Press, Inc., 1963.

HALL, WILLIAM D., ed. *Latin Pronunciation According to Roman Usage.* Tustin, Calif.: National Music Publishers, Inc., 1971.

HINES, ROBERT S. *Singer's Manual of Latin Diction and Phonetics.* New York: Macmillan Publishing Co., Inc., 1975.

JONES, ARCHIE N., M. IRVING SMITH, and ROBERT B. WALLS. *Pronouncing Guide to French, German, Italian, and Spanish.* New York: Carl Fischer, Inc., 1945.

MARIETTA, SISTER. *Singing the Liturgy.* Milwaukee: The Bruce Publishing Company, 1956.

MARSHALL, MADELEINE. *The Singer's Manual of English Diction.* New York: G. Schirmer, Inc., 1953.

MORIARTY, JOHN. *Diction.* Boston: E. C. Schirmer Music Company, 1975.

PFAUTSCH, LLOYD. *English Diction for Singers.* New York: Lawson-Gould Music Publishers, Inc., 1971.

THOMAS, CHARLES KENNETH. *Phonetics of American English.* New York: The Ronald Press Company, 1958.

Sight Singing

ADLER, SAMUEL. *Sight Singing–Pitch, Interval, Rhythm.* New York: W.W. Norton and Company, 1979.

BENWARD, BRUCE. *Sightsinging Complete,* 2nd ed. Dubuque, Iowa: William C. Brown Co., Publishers, 1973.

BERGER, MELVIN. *Fundamentals of Part Singing.* New York: Sam Fox Publishing Company, 1969.

BERKOWITZ, SOL, GABRIEL FONTRIER, and LEO KRAFT. *A New Approach to Sight Singing.* New York: W. W. Norton and Company, 1960.

COLE, SAMUEL W., and LEO R. LEWIS. *Melodia–A Comprehensive Course in Sight Singing.* Bryn Mawr, Penn.: Oliver Ditson Company, 1909.

CROWE, EDGAR, ANNIE LAWTON, and W. GILLIES WHITTAKER. *The Folk Song Sight Singing Series.* London: Oxford University Press, n.d.

DANNHÄUSER, A. *Solfège des Solfèges.* New York: G. Schirmer, Inc., 1891.

FISH, ARNOLD, and NORMAN LLOYD. *Fundamentals of Sight Singing and Ear Training.* New York: Dodd, Mead and Company, 1965.

HEFFERNAN, CHARLES W. *Teaching Children to Read Music.* New York: Appleton-Century-Crofts, 1968.

KODALY, ZOLTAN. *Let Us Sing Correctly.* London: Boosey and Hawkes, 1952.

LLOYD, NORMAN, RUTH LLOYD, and IAN DE GAETANI. *The Complete Sightsinger–A Stylistic and Historical Approach.* New York: Harper and Row, 1980.

OTTMAN, ROBERT W. *Music for Sight Singing,* 2nd ed. Englewood Cliffs, N.J.: Prentice-Hall, Inc., 1967.

Choral Technique and Artistry

*ABRAHAM, GERALD, ed. *Handel: A Symposium.* London: Oxford University Press, 1954.

*See page 119 regarding references on performance practice.

*ARNOLD, FRANK THOMAS. *The Art of Accompaniment from a Thorough-Bass.* 2 volumes. New York: Dover Publications, 1965.

BAMBERGER, CARL, ed. *The Conductor's Art.* New York: McGraw-Hill Book Company, 1965.

BENNETT, ROY C. *The Choral Singer's Handbook.* New York: Edward B. Marks Music Corporation, 1977.

*BLUME, FRIEDRICH. *Renaissance and Baroque Music: A Comprehensive Survey.* Trans. M. D. Herter Norton. New York: W. W. Norton and Company, 1967.

*————. *Two Centuries of Bach: An Account of Changing Taste.* Trans. Stanley Godman. London: Oxford University Press, 1950.

*BOULT, ADRIAN CEDRIC, and WALTER EMERY. *The St. Matthew Passion: Its Preparation and Performance.* London: Novello and Co., Ltd., 1949.

BOYD, JACK. *Rehearsal Guide for the Choral Director.* West Nyack, N.Y.: Parker Publishing Co., Inc., 1970.

*BROWN, HOWARD MAYER. *Music in the Renaissance.* Englewood Cliffs, N.J.: Prentice-Hall, Inc., 1976.

CHEYETTE, IRVING. *Tune-ups for Choral Groups.* Chicago: Hall and McCreary Company, 1950.

CHRISTENSEN, HELGA. *Better Choir Singing.* Dallas: Choristers Guild, 1973.

CHRISTIANSEN, OLAF C. *Voice Builder.* Park Ridge, Ill.: Neil A. Kjos Music Company, 1959.

COLEMAN, HENRY, and HILDA WEST. *Girls' Choirs.* London: Oxford University Press, 1962.

CONE, EDWARD T. *Musical Form and Musical Performance.* New York: W. W. Norton and Company, 1968.

COOPER, GROSVENOR, and LEONARD B. MEYER. *The Rhythmic Structure of Music.* Chicago: University of Chicago Press, 1960.

CRAIG, DON. *Twenty Choral Warmups.* New York: Plymouth Music Co., Inc., 1963.

DANN, HOLLIS. *Hollis Dann Song Series, Conductor's Book.* New York: American Book Company, 1936.

DARROW, GERALD F. *Four Decades of Choral Training.* Metuchen, N.J.: The Scarecrow Press, Inc., 1975.

*DART, THURSTON. *The Interpretation of Music.* London: Hutchinson University Library, 1967.

DAVISON, ARCHIBALD T. *Choral Conducting.* Cambridge, Mass.: Harvard University Press, 1962.

*DEAN, WINTON. *Handel's Dramatic Oratorios and Masques.* London: Oxford University Press, 1959.

DECKER, HAROLD, and JULIUS HERFORD. *Choral Conducting: A Symposium.* Englewood Cliffs, N.J.: Prentice-Hall, Inc., 1973.

*DOLMETSCH, ARNOLD. *The Interpretation of the Music of the XVII and XVIII Centuries.* London: Novello and Co., Ltd., 1946.

*DONINGTON, ROBERT. *The Interpretation of Early Music,* new version. London: Faber and Faber, 1974.

*————. *A Performer's Guide to Baroque Music.* London: Faber and Faber, 1973.

*DORIAN, FREDERICK. *The History of Music in Performance: The Art of Musical Interpretation from the Renaissance to Our Day.* New York: W. W. Norton and Company, 1966.

EBERHARDT, CARL. *A Guide to Successful Choral Rehearsals.* New York: C. F. Peters, 1973.

EHMANN, WILHELM. *Choral Directing.* Minneapolis: Augsburg Publishing House, 1968.

EHRET, WALTER. *The Choral Conductor's Handbook.* New York: Edward B. Marks Music Corporation, 1959.

EISENBERG, HELEN, and LARRY EISENBERG. *How to Lead Group Singing.* New York: Association Press, 1955.

ERICSON, ERIC, GÖSTA OHLIN, and LENNART SPANGBERG. *Choral Conducting.* New York: Walton Music Corporation, 1976.

FINN, WILLIAM J. *The Art of the Choral Conductor, Vols. I and II.* Evanston, Ill.: Summy-Birchard Publishing Company, 1960.

GARRETSON, ROBERT L. *Conducting Choral Music,* 3rd ed. Boston: Allyn and Bacon, Inc., 1970.

GORDON, LEWIS. *Choral Director's Complete Handbook.* West Nyack, N.Y.: Parker Publishing Company, Inc., 1977.

HAMPSHIRE, CYRIL. *Part Singing and Tone Blending Studies.* Scarborough, Ont., Canada: Jarman Publications Limited, 1952.

*HERZ, GERHARD. "Historical Background." *Cantata No. 4—Christ lag in Todesbanden:* J. S. Bach. Ed. Gerhard Herz. New York: W. W. Norton and Company, 1972.

*————. "Historical Background." *Cantata No. 140—Wachet auf, ruft uns die Stimme:* J. S. Bach. Ed. Gerhard Herz. New York: W. W. Norton Company, 1972.

HJORTSVANG, CARL. *The Amateur Choir Director.* New York: Abingdon-Cokesbury Press, 1941.

*HOWERTON, GEORGE. *Technique and Style in Choral Singing.* New York: Carl Fischer, Inc., 1957.

JONES, ARCHIE N. *Techniques in Choral Conducting.* Carl Fischer, Inc., 1948.

*KELLER, HERMAN. *Phrasing and Articulation: A Contribution to a Rhetoric of Music.* Trans. Leigh Gerdine. New York: W. W. Norton and Company, 1965.

KIRK, THERON W. *Choral Tone and Technic.* Westbury, N.Y.: Pro Art Publications, 1956.

KRONE, MAX T. *The Chorus and Its Conductor.* Park Ridge, Ill.: Neil A. Kjos Music Co., 1945.

LAMB, GORDON. *Choral Techniques.* Dubuque, Iowa: William C. Brown Co., Publishers, 1974.

*LARSEN, JENS PETER. *Handel's Messiah: Origins, Composition, Sources.* London: Adam and Charles Black, 1957.

LORENTZEN, BENT. *New Choral Dramatics.* New York: Walton Music Corporation, 1971.

MANSON, JOHN L. *Interpretive Choral Singing.* Nashville: Broadman Press, 1961.

McGAW, CHARLES. *Acting Is Believing.* New York: Rinehart and Company, Inc., 1955.

*MENDEL, ARTHUR. "Introduction." *The Passion According to St. John:* J. S. Bach. Ed. Arthur Mendel. New York: G. Schirmer, Inc., 1951.

*————. "Note on Performance." *Missa Brevis in F Major* (1774-K. 192): W. A. Mozart. Ed. Arthur Mendel. New York: G. Schirmer, Inc., 1955.

*————. "Preface." *A German Requiem:* Heinrich Schütz. Ed. Arthur Mendel. New York: G. Schirmer, Inc., 1957.

*————. "Remarks on the Performance of The Christmas Story." *The Christmas Story:* Heinrich Schütz. Ed. Arthur Mendel. New York: G. Schirmer, Inc., 1949.

MOE, DANIEL. *Basic Choral Concepts.* Minneapolis: Augsburg Publishing House, 1972.

————. *Problems in Conducting.* Minneapolis: Augsburg Publishing House, 1973.

*NEUMANN, FREDERICK. *Ornamentation in Baroque and Post-Baroque Music.* Princeton, N.J.: Princeton University Press, 1978.

*See page 119 regarding references on performance practice.

PELOQUIN, C. ALEXANDER. *Choral Precision.* Toledo: Gregorian Institute of America, 1962.

PFAUTSCH, LLOYD. *Mental Warmups for the Choral Director.* New York: Lawson-Gould Music Publishers, Inc., 1969.

POOLER, FRANK, and BRENT PIERCE. *New Choral Notation.* New York: Walton Music Corporation, 1971.

POOLER, FRANK, and GAIL L. SHOUP. *Choralography.* New York: Walton Music Corporation, 1975.

*ROBERTSON, ALEC. *Requiem: Music of Mourning and Consolation.* New York: Praeger, 1967.

ROBINSON, RAY, and ALLEN WINOLD. *The Choral Experience: Literature, Materials, and Methods.* New York: Harper and Row, Publishers, Inc., 1976.

ROE, PAUL F. *Choral Music Education.* Englewood Cliffs, N.J.: Prentice-Hall, Inc., 1970.

*ROSEN, CHARLES. *The Classical Style.* New York: W. W. Norton and Company, 1972.

*ROTHSCHILD, FRITZ. *The Lost Tradition in Music.* London: Adam and Charles Black, 1953.

*———. *Musical Performance in the Times of Mozart and Beethoven.* London: Adam and Charles Black, 1961.

*———. *Stress and Movement in the Works of J. S. Bach.* London: Adam and Charles Black, 1966.

ROWEN, RUTH HALLE. *Music Through Sources and Documents.* Englewood Cliffs, N.J.: Prentice-Hall, Inc., 1979.

SATEREN, LELAND B. *Criteria for Judging Choral Music and Those Straight-Tone Choirs.* Minneapolis: Augsburg Publishing House, 1963.

———. *Focus on Mixed Meter Music and Line in Choral Music.* Minneapolis: Augsburg Publishing House, 1968.

SCARMOLIN, LOUIS A. *The Chorister's Daily Dozen.* Westbury, N.Y.: Pro Art Publications, 1951.

SCOTT, RICHARD. *Sevenfold Choral Method.* Minneapolis: Handy-Folio Music Company, n.d.

*SHAW, WATKINS. *A Textual and Historical Companion to Handel's "Messiah."* London: Novello and Co., Ltd., 1965.

SIMON, BILL. *Warm Up and Sing.* New York: Carl Fischer, Inc., 1959.

STANTON, ROYAL. *The Dynamic Choral Conductor.* Delaware Water Gap, Penn.: Shawnee Press, Inc., 1971.

STONE, LEONARD. *Chorus Builder.* Rockville Centre, N.Y.: Belwin, Inc., 1962.

*STRUNK, OLIVER. *Source Readings in Music History from Classical Antiquity through the Romantic Era.* New York: W. W. Norton and Company, 1950.

SUNDERMAN, LLOYD FREDERICK. *Choral Organization and Administration.* Rockville Centre, N.Y.: Belwin, Inc., 1954.

*TERRY, CHARLES SANFORD. *Bach: The Mass in B Minor,* 2nd ed. London: Oxford University Press, 1956.

THOMAS, KURT. *The Choral Conductor.* New York: Associated Music Publishers, 1971.

*TOVEY, DONALD FRANCIS. *Essays in Musical Analysis, Vol. V: Vocal Music.* London: Oxford University Press, 1956.

VAN CAMP, LEONARD. *Choral Warm-ups for Minds, Ears, and Voices.* New York: Lawson-Gould Music Publishers, Inc., 1972.

WARING, FRED. *Tone Syllables.* Delaware Water Gap, Penn.: Shawnee Press, Inc., 1951.

*WERNER, JACK. *Mendelssohn's "Elijah": A Historical and Analytical Guide to the Oratorio.* London: Chappell, 1965.

*WHITTAKER, W. GILLIES. *The Cantatas of Johann Sebastian Bach.* 2 volumes. London: Oxford University Press, 1959.

WILSON, HARRY ROBERT. *Artistic Choral Singing.* New York: G. Schirmer, Inc., 1959.

WOODS, GLENN H. *Ensemble Intonation.* Beaumont, Calif.: Pallma Music Products Corp., 1937.

Repertoire

BURNSWORTH, CHARLES C. *Choral Music for Women's Voices: An Annotated Bibliography of Recommended Works.* Metuchen, N.J.: The Scarecrow Press, Inc., 1968.

CHARLES, SYDNEY ROBINSON. *A Handbook of Music and Music Literature in Sets and Series.* New York: The Free Press, 1972.

DUCKLES, VINCENT, comp. *Music Reference and Research Materials: An Annotated Bibliography,* 3rd ed. New York: The Free Press, 1974.

FELLOWS, EDMUND H. *The English Madrigal School: A Guide to Its Practical Use.* London: Stainer and Bell Ltd., n.d.

HEYER, ANNA HARRIET, comp. *Historical Sets, Collected Editions, and Monuments of Music,* 2nd ed. Chicago: American Library Association, 1969.

JACOBS, ARTHUR, ed. *Choral Music: A Symposium.* Baltimore: Penguin Books, 1963.

KJELSON, LEE, and JAMES McCRAY. *The Singer's Manual of Choral Music Literature.* Melville, N.Y.: Belwin Mills Publishing Corp., 1973.

LIEF, ARTHUR. *The Choral Art, Vols. I and II.* New York: Lawson-Gould Music Publishers, Inc., 1974.

MAY, JAMES D. *Avant-Garde Choral Music: An Annotated Selected Bibliography.* Metuchen, N.J.: The Scarecrow Press, Inc., 1977.

NARDONE, THOMAS R., JAMES H. NYE, and MARK RESNICK. *Choral Music in Print, Volumes I and II, and 1976 Supplement.* Philadelphia: Musicadata, Inc., 1974 and 1976.

ROBINSON, RAY, ed. *Choral Music.* New York: W. W. Norton and Company, 1978.

TORTOLANO, WILLIAM. *Original Music for Men's Voices: A Selected Bibliography.* Metuchen, N.J.: The Scarecrow Press, Inc., 1973.

ULRICH, HOMER. *A Survey of Choral Music.* New York: Harcourt Brace Jovanovich, Inc., 1973.

YOUNG, PERCY M. *The Choral Tradition.* New York: W. W. Norton and Company, 1962.

INDEX